SEA KAYAKING
ROUGH WATERS

BY ALEX MATTHEWS

D0721378

SEA KAYAKING
ROUGH WATERS

BY ALEX MATTHEWS

PHOTOS BY PAUL VILLECOURT & JOCK BRADLEY

THP THE HELICONIA PRESS

Published by

 THE HELICONIA PRESS

1576 Beachburg Road
Beachburg, Ontario K0J 1C0
www.helipress.com

Copyright © 2006 The Heliconia Press
All rights reserved. No part of this book may be reproduced in any form, or by any electronic,
mechanical, digital, or other means, without permission in writing from the publisher.

This book was printed in Singapore

First Edition

ISBN # 978-1-896980-26-3

Written by: Alex Matthews
Photography by: Jock Bradley & Paul Villecourt
Illustrations by: Paul Mason
Design and Layout: Robyn Hader
Edited by: Ken Whiting & Rebecca Sandiford

Library and Archives Canada Cataloguing in Publication

Matthews, Alex, 1964-

Sea kayaking : rough waters / by Alex Matthews ; photography
by Jock Bradley and Paul Villecourt ; edited by Rebecca Sandiford

ISBN 978-1-896980-26-3

1. Sea kayaking. I. Sandiford, Rebecca, 1973- II. Title.

GV788.5.M383 2007   797.1'224   C2006-905066-X

About Safety

Kayaking is an activity with inherent risks, and this book is
designed as a general guide, not a substitute for experience.
The publisher and the author do not take responsibility for
the use of any of the materials or methods described in this
book. By following any of the procedures described within,
you do so at your own risk.

TABLE OF CONTENTS

ACKNOWLEDGEMENTS

In a sense, this book has been many years in the making. It's just one of the byproducts of the time that I've spent playing on the sea and honing the skills needed to better meet and enjoy the challenges of traveling across rough water in a small self-propelled craft. My journey has certainly not been a lonely one – I have met many wonderful people who have contributed valuable insights, shared warmth and laughter, and helped me on my way.

Foremost, I would like to thank my beautiful wife Rochelle, who not only indulges my fascination with kayaking, but is also wise enough to actually send me out to paddle when I'm restless from being dry for too long.

Thanks to Mum and Dad (Rosemary and Roy) for giving me more than I can ever thank them for. Thanks go out to Spike Gladwin, a good friend who has contributed many hours discussing the finer points of kayak design, construction and performance.

I'd also like to send my sincere thanks to those who have provided ongoing support to our projects and who played a significant role in making this book a reality. Thanks go to Nando Zucchi and Sara Knies of Necky Kayaks, Craig Langford and Joe Matuska of Aquabound Paddles, Chris Jacobs of Extrasport, Morgan Goldie of North Water, Mike Patterson and Rich Wilson of Snap Dragon, Lisa Beckstead, Marta Miller and Michael Duffy of Kokatat, and Mike May of Brunton.

Thank you Jock Bradley and Paul Villecourt—two truly gifted photographers who go to just about any length to bring back the best shots possible, rain or shine!

Finally, a very big thank you to Ken Whiting for instigating this project (since without Ken this book would not exist) and for giving it a home at The Heliconia Press. Thanks also to the whole THP crew: Robyn Hader, Rebecca Sandiford, Lisa Utronki, Ruth Gordon and Nicole Whiting.

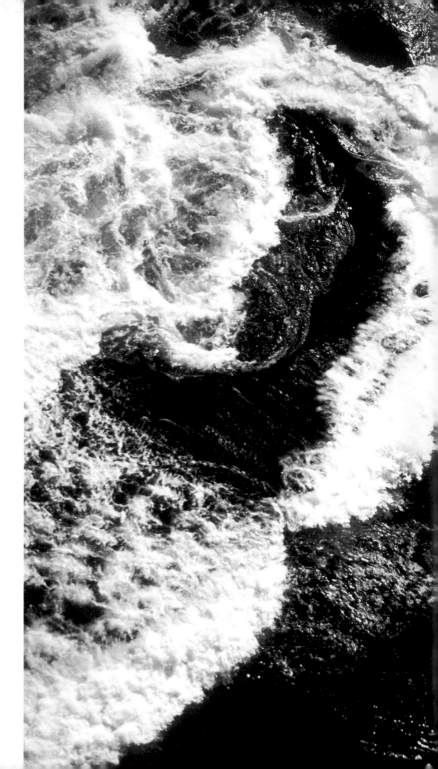

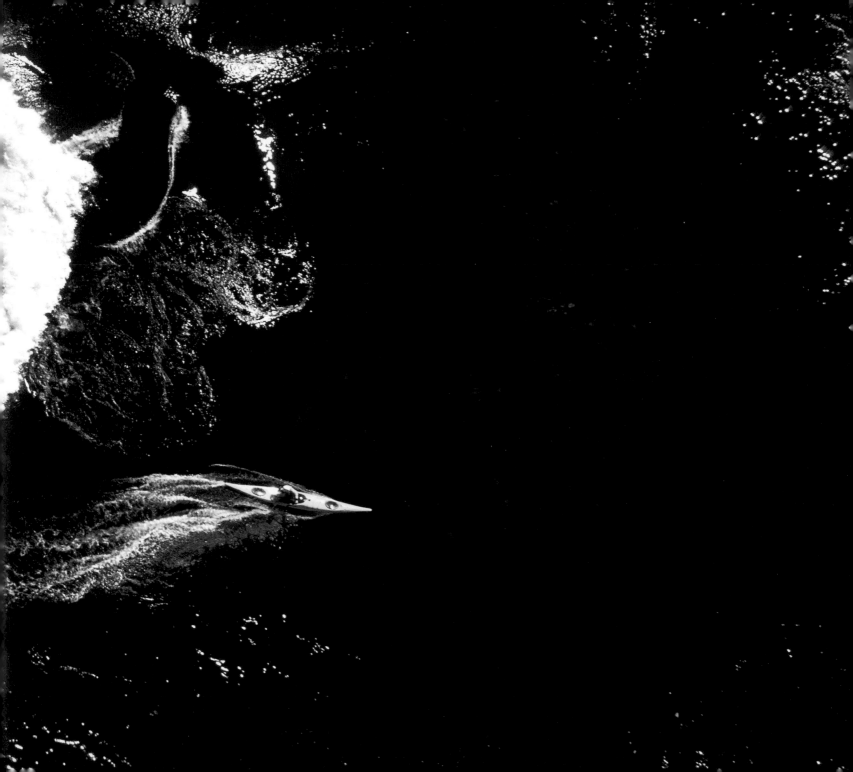

INTRODUCTION TO ROUGH WATER PADDLING

In the early days of cartography, there were vast expanses of the oceans and coasts that were uncharted. The world was thought to be flat, and falling off the edge was a very real fear. After all, many ships left port only to disappear forever. When a mapmaker drew up a chart and no information was available for a given area, the perils of the unknown were summed up with the words "here be dragons", written in the map's blank spaces—where knowledge failed and where the world, it seemed, ended.

Dragons! The early mapmaker's idea is actually not far off, metaphorically. While the sea slumbers, we can venture over the shiny skins, traveling almost anywhere we choose to explore. But when the ocean stirs, and the dragons begin to rouse from their sleep, it is unwise to seek to tame them. With respect and knowledge, they might let us play with them for a time, but once the beasts are fully awake, riding their backs is nothing short of insane.

Sea kayaking in rough water can be an absolute blast. There's nothing quite like picking up a good surf ride or swooping through current into an eddy. Learning the skills necessary for paddling in rough conditions is also a great way to build solid "real world" skills that will improve your comfort level and take your paddling to new heights, even if you have no intention of paddling regularly in challenging conditions.

While rougher conditions can be a lot of fun, venturing out to play is also a serious exercise in sound judgment. The line between safely having fun and getting in over your head can sometimes be a fine one. Sea kayaking the open coast or venturing into strong currents, tidal rips and waves demands serious preparation and an acceptance of the real risks involved. Strong boat handling skills are absolutely essential, as is a positive mental attitude, appropriate gear and a good support team. It's also important to adopt a conservative approach and to heed the little voice in your head that counsels common sense. If you're reading this book, it probably means that you're interested in gathering knowledge that will help you paddle more confidently and competently in challenging conditions. Although this is an important step to take, it's even more important to learn and practice these skills in a controlled environment. Taking a course from a professional instructor is invaluable for this reason, and should be considered a prerequisite before venturing out on your own. Kayak schools and paddling clubs are also great places to meet other paddlers, and anyone who has spent time sea kayaking can tell you that one of the greatest things about the sport is the people that you meet, and the opportunity it provides to build friendships. Another great way to hone your rough water paddling is to try whitewater kayaking. The skills you learn and the confidence you'll gain from learning to deal with river rapids and current will be a huge asset when the going gets rough while sea kayaking.

Whether you're looking to paddle in more challenging conditions, or looking to learn new skills and build confidence for sheltered paddling, it is my hope that *Sea Kayaking: Rough Waters* helps you reach your goals, because for me, there is nothing more exciting than to learn and to share my learning experience with others.

photo: Rochelle Relyea

ABOUT THE AUTHOR

ALEX MATTHEWS

Alex Matthews is a passionate sea kayaker, whitewater paddler and kayak-surfer. He has guided sea kayak trips in many areas around Vancouver Island, the Queen Charlottes, and Baja, Mexico. He has explored sections of both the West and East Coasts of Canada and the United States. A successful writer known for his irreverent wit and humor, his articles have appeared in many prominent paddlesports publications, and he has worked in both kayak design and marketing for prominent paddlesport companies. His abiding fascination for any liquid environment, and the ocean in particular, fuels his zeal for crafts that interact with water as directly as possible. It is no surprise that his sign of the Zodiac is Pisces – the sign of the fish.

photo: Jill Sokolec

photo: Alex Matthews

PHOTOGRAPHERS

JOCK BRADLEY

Whether bushwhacking through Philippine jungles, rappelling into vertical gorges or diving deep into ocean depths, Jock consistently overcomes tremendous obstacles to obtain the perfect shot. It is, above all, this type of dedication and work ethic that sets him apart—making him one of the world's foremost professional outdoor photographers. For more info, visit www.jockbradley.com.

PAUL VILLECOURT

Paul Villecourt is a French photographer and paddler dedicated to capturing the sensations of adventure and outdoor sports. His passion for paddling has taken him and his camera to all corners of the world. Paul is regarded as one of the finest outdoor photographers in the world, and his work has been featured in virtually every outdoor magazine in Europe and North America. For more info, visit www.outdoor-reporter.com.

1

ROUGH WATER ESSENTIALS

WARMING UP AND GENERAL CONDITIONING THE MENTAL GAME
EQUIPMENT THE PADDLE PERSONAL GEAR

WARMING UP AND GENERAL CONDITIONING

A fit paddler is a better paddler

Without a doubt, your body is your most important piece of paddling equipment. Your body is the engine that will power your kayak forward, so just as you would for your car engine you'll want to do some maintenance to keep things running smoothly.

Warm up before paddling, and stretch. It's obvious to stretch the arms and upper body, but don't forget about your lower body. In a kayak, you sit with your legs straight out in front of you, with knees slightly flexed. Tight hamstrings will make this sitting position awkward and uncomfortable, and will impact your performance. Although sea kayaking can be a very low impact sport, in challenging water, the simple truth is that the stronger and more flexible you are, the more comfortable and confident you'll be.

There is no substitute for power and conditioning when punching big waves or racking up long days in rough conditions. Being fit will keep you warmer, safer, and let you have more fun. A fit paddler is a better paddler.

THE MENTAL GAME

Good paddling technique and a high level of fitness will go an awfully long way in harsh conditions. But there are other less tangible elements that will dictate the quality of your paddling performance and influence how much fun you have on the water.

Your mental attitude has a huge impact on your ability to successfully navigate rough water. In any challenging situation, a positive mental attitude is a huge asset. By staying positive, good things happen. You'll have more fun, be more fun to be around and actually perform much better too! When making decisions on the water, it's never a bad idea to be conservative and opt for

Regular stretching increases flexibility and leads to greater comfort in a kayak.

the safest and surest route. This sometimes means avoiding surf, swinging out wide around a rip current, paddling channels at slack tide or choosing not to paddle at all. But if, after considering all the conditions and factors, you decide to "go for it", do so with a positive outlook and confidence. One thing that I have learned time and again, is that paddling aggressively and with commitment will see me through the "tricky bits" far better than a tentative, timid approach. Half measures usually yield half results.

It's a lot easier to gauge where your physical skills are at, but it's very important that you take the time to consider how your mental game is going. Remember that the goal is to have fun in one of Mother Nature's most incredible natural playgrounds, and to do so safely. It is the truly confident paddler who has no problem making the decision to avoid a given feature, or even forgo paddling altogether, in favor of spending the day on shore, safely watching the sea.

EQUIPMENT

The Kayak

When considering what kayak to take into rough water, you need to consider several key issues: flotation, durability, fit, and handling characteristics. It's important to note that if your kayak has weaknesses in any of these areas, it will likely have an effect on both your confidence and your actual ability to navigate harsh conditions.

Of course there are some standard safety features that any kayak should have, such as perimeter lines to help during rescues, and a sensible shock cord layout that makes carrying a spare paddle and charts easy. Also essential are waterproof hatches that won't fail even when loaded by a dumping wave or a paddler crawling across them.

Anatomy of a Kayak

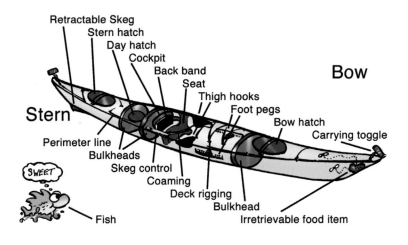

Flotation

Just as a paddler requires flotation in the form of a life jacket, a kayak must have flotation as well. Without adequate flotation, a boat will actually sink when swamped. Watching your kayak fill with water and then disappear beneath the waves must be the worst feeling in the world.

The best way to achieve flotation in a kayak is with built-in waterproof walls called bulkheads. Bulkheads separate the kayak's interior volume into separate, waterproof sections. They also introduce a lot of structural strength to a kayak, increasing deck stiffness and increasing the boat's resistance to crushing. There should be at least two bulkheads, one in front of the cockpit and one behind the cockpit, but many kayaks will have three or more bulkheads. This provides your kayak with added flotation in the event that one of the sealed flotation compartments is breached. Ideally, the stern bulkhead should be positioned very close to the back edge of the coaming and the bow bulkhead should be positioned just forward of the paddler's feet. This reduces the volume of water that can flood the cockpit which makes both

To maintain flotation, check and seal all hatches before departure.

rescues and paddling a swamped kayak easier. This is particularly important when paddling in rough water, since it is not unheard of for crashing waves to pop a paddler's spray deck, or for a swimmer to re-enter a swamped kayak and paddle it full until an opportunity to bail it out arises.

Bulkheads must be completely "bombproof" and remain bonded in the boat no matter what. Failure of a bulkhead means loss of flotation. A kayak with only one intact bulkhead may float in a vertical position, making rescue a serious challenge or even impossible when the conditions are really rough.

In composite kayaks, the strongest bulkheads are composite ones that are glassed in place. In plastic kayaks, plastic bulkheads that are welded in place are the most durable. Foam bulkheads are quite common and can also work well, but you'll want to keep a close eye on them to make sure that they stay glued firmly in place and remain waterproof. For any type of bulkhead, a marine sealant is used to fill any gaps between the shell of the boat and the bulkhead.

Curved bulkheads are more complicated to manufacture and install, but have the benefit of spreading stress loads over a wider surface. This results in fewer cracks and fractures in the gelcoat around bulkhead locations when a kayak is subjected to crushing forces or impacts.

The hatches, which allow entry into the individual flotation compartments, are another potential weak point when it comes to preserving the integrity of your craft. In other words, they tend to leak. There are many different hatch designs on the market. For general paddling, most work well, but for rough water paddling, you'll want a hatch cover that provides the driest seal possible. Systems that use rigid shell covers that snap overtop of hatches are least likely to be blown open or be ripped off by breaking waves. Whichever system you choose, be sure to inspect it regularly for wear that might reduce its effectiveness. It's also important that you physically check that hatches are fully secured before setting off. Don't assume that your hatches are "good to go" just because they were the last time you went paddling. Check them. Check your paddling partner's hatches too. This is a real world safety concern and should become an instinctive habit. In rough water, you really don't want to have to deal with a compromised hatch, let alone a fully flooded flotation compartment!

Tandem kayaks should have at least three bulkheads, and those with center hatches will often have four. The goals are the same: to minimize the volume of water that can flood the interior of the kayak, and to provide buoyancy in the form of sealed, waterproof cargo compartments.

Folding kayaks and traditional skin boats do not employ bulkheads in their construction. Sea-socks and float-bags are required to create flotation in these instances. A sea-sock is basically a large waterproof bag (usually made out of coated nylon) that fits tightly around the cockpit coaming and extends into the boat.

The sea sock is contoured to fit the lower half of a paddler, so a kayaker can comfortably sit in the sock. If the kayak capsizes, water will only enter the sock, but not the whole volume of the kayak. To empty a swamped boat, the sock is hauled out while still attached to the coaming, and flipped inside out, draining the water. It can then be stuffed back into the boat, and the paddler can re-enter.

Float bags can also be a valuable tool for displacing water in kayaks without bulkheads. Float bags are watertight inflatable bladders that are shaped to fit inside a kayak. Once inflated, these bags will occupy a lot of space inside a boat and dramatically decrease the volume of water that can flow into the craft. The resulting air pockets provide important buoyancy. Always be sure to securely fasten float bags in place because they have an uncanny ability to escape the confines of a boat, especially in tumbling

Spot the duct tape field repair to the bow?
Paddling off Money Point, Cape Breton, Canada.

surf or swirling current. If they aren't tied in, and simply float free, float bags won't generate any of the essential buoyancy that they are designed to provide. Float bags can also provide insurance in boats equipped with bulkheads. In the event that the hull is breached, a float bag will minimize the water that can enter and provide flotation.

A good mantra to repeat before heading into gnarly water is: "flotation, flotation, flotation". This refers to your PFD of course, but it should also extend to your and your partners' boats. In the event of a swim, or a blown spray deck, it really is disheartening to have your kayak sink to the bottom of the ocean. Always ensure

that your kayak has lots of buoyancy in the form of large volumes of trapped air at both ends of the boat.

Durability

Simply put, it is important that a kayak stand up to the rigors and conditions that it will encounter. Therefore for the purposes of rough water paddling, you should have a kayak that can withstand pounding surf, crashing seas, and even the occasional collision with rocks and other unforgiving surfaces.

Plastic or polymer kayaks are amazingly impact-resistant and deal with full-on abuse incredibly well. If you paddle in very rocky areas, drag your boat, or spend much time paddling in areas with ice, then plastic is definitely the way to go.

Composite kayaks are stiffer, hold their shape better, and are significantly lighter. For my money, they also 'feel' much sweeter in the water. And while they won't put up with endless amounts of actual abuse, composite kayaks are much tougher than most people suspect. Bear in mind that there is often a direct correlation between weight and durability. If a composite boat is ultra lightweight, there is bound to be some trade-off in durability. I have had the best success, relative to durability, with fiberglass kayaks in the 55 lbs (25 kg) and above weight range.

Pre-trip preparation is also very important. Before getting on the water, be sure to inspect for and deal with any damage or wear that your kayak may have sustained. This is not only restricted to damage to the structural integrity of the hull or deck, but should include all aspects of your kayak. Deal with wear before it becomes a serious problem. The failure of other parts of a boat can have potentially terrible consequences. A loose back-band, broken thigh brace, leaky bulkhead or cracked combing can all lead to a seriously compromised level of performance.

Fit

When paddling in challenging conditions you need to give yourself whatever edge you can—so make sure that you are wearing your kayak, and not just sitting in it. Your goal should be to establish a snug but comfortable fit. A proper fit in your kayak will make a major difference to how the boat responds to your movements. Your kayak's cockpit needs to serve as the interface between your body and your boat. In the same way that a snug, well-fitting ski boot can effectively transfer the power and control from your legs and body to a pair of skis, so must the fit of your kayak effectively transfer input from your hips, knees and legs directly to the boat. Unlike a ski boot though, your kayak must fit loosely enough that you can get in or out of it with relative ease.

A snug fit is essential to confident edging.

Paddling through small surf, Acadia National Park, Maine, USA.

The seating position in a kayak provides four important points of contact with the boat: these are the butt, hips, thighs, and feet. To maximize interface with a boat, it's important to get all four points of contact working for you.

There are as many seat designs available as there are kayaks, and because each and every one of our butts sport their very own distinct shape, finding a seat that fits you best is truly a personal pilgrimage. A seat does two things. Obviously, it provides a place to park your backside, but it also serves to hold you in place in the boat. The seat alone doesn't lock you in, but it prevents you from sliding backward or side-to-side.

The contours of the seat pan and the seat back or back-band prevent any movement backward in the boat. The seat back or back-band also provides very desirable back support. It needs to be low enough that it doesn't interfere with leaning back or torso rotation. The back support should be snug against the lower back, encouraging an erect sitting position, and an active posture.

The seat must also provide contact with your hips—or a place

Don't hesitate to customize the fit of your kayak by gluing in foam. Closed cell foam is a wonderful material that absorbs no water, is easily shaped, and provides a firm yet pliant surface to press against. To glue foam into place, aggressively sand the surfaces of both the boat and the foam before gluing pads in with contact cement. You can then shape the foam to a custom fit with a serrated knife, sandpaper or a Sureform. All outfitting should be very secure, even when subjected to the effects of pounding waves and current. Having to re-enter a kayak with a severely compromised fit is not what any paddler wants, especially in heavy seas. Spots that benefit from added foam include the thigh hooks, hip pads, and seat. Some folks like foam under their heels, and extending the seat pan will provide more support under the leg and will often cure the dreaded pins and needles sensation that accompanies one's legs "falling asleep".

Pedal systems in kayaks are designed to adjust fore and aft, so they can accommodate paddlers of widely varying leg lengths. When seated in your kayak, the balls of your feet need to be firmly planted on the pedals, with your legs flexed and knees tucked under the deck.

Handling Characteristics & Suitability for Rough Water

What each individual paddler desires in their personal kayak will differ in every case, but certain characteristics in a boat will make paddling in rough conditions easier.

Exposure to Wind

Low profile kayaks with low decks will generally yield a nice snug fit that will provide the best interface between a kayak and paddler. Low decks also present very little surface area for wind to act upon. A low profile will help a kayak perform better when strong winds are encountered. A kayak should also "weathercock" or turn into the wind, but this should be a modest effect that is

Catching a surf ride on a boat's wake.

to glue your own custom hip pads. Hip pads will prevent sliding side-to-side and help transfer energy from your hips to the kayak. A sloppy fit in the hips reduces the ease and effectiveness of edging. Again, the fit should be snug, but not so tight that the pelvis is totally locked in place.

Good thigh hooks provide an incredible amount of contact with the boat and are the most critical component of outfitting relative to boat control. They should be contoured to fit the top of your leg and hooked aggressively enough that your leg isn't likely to slip out from under the thigh brace. Placement of the thigh hooks is also very personal, and some designs offer an adjustable system so thigh support can be modified for different fits.

A fit paddler is a better paddler – Ken puts on the power.

easily balanced out by deploying a skeg, rudder or by simply edging the kayak and sweeping with the paddle.

Maneuverability

One of the biggest factors affecting your kayak's handling is its rocker profile. Rocker is the curvature of the hull as viewed from the side. The more rocker a kayak has, the more easily it will turn, and the less effectively it will "track", or travel in a straight line. When playing in rock gardens, current, surf and in other tight spaces, I prefer a boat with a large amount of rocker.

Stability

When we talk about a boat's stability there are usually two aspects that get discussed: initial stability and secondary stability.

TIP

My preferred rough water kayak has plenty of rocker, plenty of volume in the ends, and a fairly wide beam. The rocker and width provides a maneuverable and stable platform, while the volume in the ends of the kayak encourages the ends to stay near or return to the surface quickly—a great feature when dealing with surf and other large waves. An "undernourished", or low-volume bow is a real detriment in waves because it will often plunge out of sight, or "submarine" beneath the surface—where it can be pushed in any direction with a lot of force by waves and current.

Initial stability refers to how stable a kayak feels when sitting flat on the water. This is most affected by the width of a kayak and its cross-sectional shape. An initially stable boat will typically be wider and flatter on the bottom than other kayaks.

Secondary stability refers to how stable a kayak feels when tilted on edge. Ideally the kayak will feel comfortable throughout the full range of edging. Secondary stability is most affected by the cross-sectional shape of the kayak. The more narrow and rounded the hull of a kayak is, the easier it will be to get on edge and hold there. A kayak with a wide, flat hull will usually be harder to hold on edge, although it will have good initial stability.

Convenience

A final issue to consider are niceties such as recessed deck fittings and hatches. A well-designed fore deck with recessed fittings will generally throw a lot less spray up when waves wash over your deck. Recessed deck fittings also present less of a hazard for tearing soft wet skin or bashing knuckles.

THE PADDLE

Your paddle is your most direct connection to the water. It drives you forward, makes you stop, helps you turn and stay upright... the list goes on. To use another automotive analogy, if you are the engine, then your paddle is the driveshaft. In fact, it's also the wheels. And the tires, and the brakes, and the steering wheel, and column, and roll bar and... well, you get the picture. The kayak paddle is such an essential piece of gear that we carry two complete sets of them: a primary paddle, and a spare, just in case something goes wrong. Now that says something about the overwhelming importance of paddles.

Paddles are built from a variety of materials like plastic, fiberglass, carbon or wood. Plastic blades offer a great blend of performance and affordability. Fiberglass and carbon paddles are lighter and stiffer, but cost significantly more. Wood paddles feel nice in-hand, but generally require more maintenance and care than synthetic materials.

NOTE

You always require two paddles. One will travel on the deck as a spare, in case your primary paddle is lost or damaged. The two paddles need not be the same, but the spare must be good enough that you will feel confident using it in the nastiest conditions.

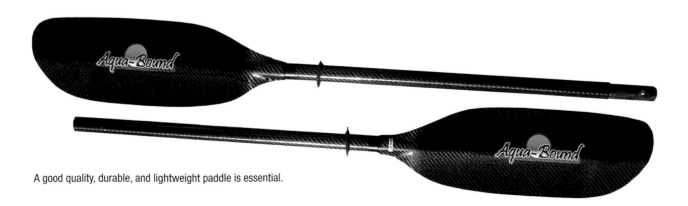

A good quality, durable, and lightweight paddle is essential.

Regardless of the material you choose, do not scrimp on the purchase of your paddle. At sea, the failure of this essential piece of gear is an incredibly alarming situation and one to be avoided at all costs. Demo as many paddles as you can and spend the money to buy a model from a well-established brand that has a good reputation for durability.

A wide variety of paddle lengths and blade sizes and shapes are available. For the purpose of rough water paddling, a shorter overall length is best because it promotes a more active "high angle" paddling posture. I am just under six feet tall, and I prefer to use a paddle between 210cm and 215cm. Ken is almost six feet, three inches, and he prefers a paddle between 220 and 230 cm.

As for the size of the paddle blades, quite simply, the smaller the blade, the less bite it will have, and the easier it will be to draw through the water. The bigger the blade, the more resistance and power it will generate. Long, skinny blades, with small surface areas, are preferred for long distance paddling where a "high cadence and low resistance" formula will yield a more mellow cruising speed. For rough water, a wider, squarer blade with more of a "cupped" cross-sectional shape is better because it grabs more water and provides the support needed to accelerate and change directions quickly, which can make a big difference in turbulent and dynamic water. The stronger you are, the larger the paddle blades and the longer the shaft you'll be able to control.

With regards to the offset or feather of the blades on your paddle, one nice thing is that most sea kayak paddles have two-piece shafts, with a center ferrule that allows this to be adjusted. The amount of feather for a paddle is a very personal choice and will depend on each individual's preference.

I personally favor a lower degree of feather in the 45 degree and under range. Higher degrees of feather demand more bending of the wrist, which can put far more strain on the wrist and forearm. The debate over the advantages and disadvantages of different feather angles is endless. When paddling into a very strong headwind, a 90 degree feather will allow the top blade to slice through the wind, making your forward stroke more efficient. But consider the same degree of feather relative to a beam (side) wind, and suddenly that top blade is angled into the wind, acting as a weathervane and trying to topple you over with every gust. The fact is that there is simply no single "correct" feather angle. A 45 degree sheds almost as much wind as a 90 and requires less flexing of the wrist; 30 works well too. For the record, both Ken and I paddle unfeathered, as do traditional Inuit and Greenland paddlers. So pick a feather that feels good for you and your body, and stick with it until you have a really good reason to change.

Some paddles have bent or "ergo(nomic) shafts". Their goal is to lessen wrist and muscle fatigue by placing the joints of the hand and wrist in a more natural position when taking a stroke. Because of the added complexity of the manufacture of the shaft, these paddles are usually quite costly. Although their true value is a subject of great debate, we believe that the answer is a very personal thing. What works for one person may not work for another, so be sure to try before you buy.

Paddle Leashes

A paddle leash can be a handy piece of gear. If wet exiting, a leash will keep the paddle with the boat or paddler, allowing the swimmer to focus all their effort on corralling their kayak and not worrying about locating their paddle. A leash is also useful when performing rescues, teaching, taking photos, or any other task requiring both hands. With a leash, you can drop your paddle anytime, without fear of losing it. It may sound silly, but even in broad daylight and calm conditions, it can be surprisingly difficult to spot and retrieve an errant paddle that has floated only a short distance away from its owner. In rough conditions, a paddle can simply disappear in seconds, never to be seen again.

There are basically two types of leashes: those that attach the paddle to the paddler, and those that attach the paddle to the boat. The best leashes are very compact and simple designs. They can be rolled up around the shaft when not in use, or stored in a corner of a PFD pocket.

A paddle leash frees up both hands and prevents paddle loss.

One place to avoid the use of a paddle leash is in the surf zone, due to the potential danger of getting yourself, your paddle, or both tangled in the leash.

Whether you choose to use a leash or not, it's obvious that the number one line of defense against losing a paddle is a firm and secure grip on the shaft. You don't need to "white knuckle" it with a death grip, but when the wind is howling, or the ocean is pitching, a fairly tight grip isn't out of place. After all, if we keep with the automotive analogy, losing your paddle in rough seas is comparable to getting four simultaneous flat tires while driving on the freeway.

PERSONAL GEAR

Your gear's job is very simply to allow you to paddle to the very best of your abilities, and to have the most fun doing it. To accomplish this goal, gear must help keep you safe, warm, allow a full range of movement, stand up to abuse well, and be as versatile as possible.

Something to keep in mind is that as you improve as a paddler, your need for good quality paddling gear grows. For example, the better you get, the less likely you are to flip and need to wet exit. If you're a good paddler who needs to wet exit, chances are quite good that it's because you're in a fairly severe situation with potentially significant consequences. Having good gear in these circumstances could make an enormous difference.

Quality construction and top notch materials do not result in bargain basement prices. While the paddlesports industry operates in a highly competitive marketplace, you do get what you pay for. Very seldom, if ever, have I regretted buying a superior piece of gear, regardless of cost. Spend the money, and buy the gear that will get the job done. You will be more comfortable, happier, safer, and you will likely perform better.

PFD

Because paddling in rough water can be physically challenging, and may require energetically explosive and dynamic movements, it is important that your PFD not restrict your range of motion in any way. At the same time, it must fit snugly, so it stays in place and will not "ride up". A PFD must also have plenty of flotation in case you do find yourself swimming in rough conditions. Once you're relegated to swimming for survival, your lifejacket will be a key piece of survival gear.

When selecting a PFD, choose one that is approved by the coastguard for your area. It should be short in the torso so that it's comfortable for sitting in a boat. Kayaking-specific models strike a great balance between flotation and low-profile designs. The result is a vest that won't obstruct movement, but will reliably keep you afloat. By keeping the bulkiest part of the PFD low on the torso, away from the shoulders and upper chest, a great range of motion can be preserved.

Your PFD should fit you very snugly when cinched down, and yet still be really comfortable. A quick and easy test on dry land is to haul up on the shoulder straps to make sure that the jacket is staying in place. Try swimming a big tidal rapid or get truly worked in the surf, and you will quickly appreciate the need for a PFD that stays in place no matter what.

A good PFD provides flotation and a secure fit, without impeding movement.

Fashion is fine, but when it comes to safety, the louder the color, the better, so pick a PFD in orange, red, yellow or hot pink and be seen! In big seas, confused conditions or standing on the beach after destroying your kayak in the surf, you'll want to stand out visually. Many designs feature reflective trim, which is great, especially in low light situations.

It's also very handy to have a couple of pockets that will securely hold things like a VHF radio, a snack, or a warm hat. There should be a spot for a whistle as well. Some vests have anchor points for strobes and hydration packs; the latter is an especially good option.

Rescue PFDs come equipped with integrated tow-system belts, which are excellent for towing over both long and short distances. Integrated tow systems should all feature quick-release buckles so that the towline can be disconnected in an instant. This is a very important safety feature because it is imperative that a rescuer be able to quickly escape the tow line if it gets tangled. Before using any tow system, it's a good idea to seek instruction in its proper use. Towlines can introduce serious hazards, particularly when deployed in dynamic conditions like surf or current.

Spray Skirt/Spray Deck

A good spray skirt (also called, and generally referred to in this book as a spray deck) is an absolutely essential piece of gear for rough water paddling. The failure of a spray deck in rough conditions represents a serious situation. Alone in big seas or current, it can be next to impossible to get a deck back on once it has popped. Flooding the cockpit of a boat severely compromises its handling characteristics and puts the paddler at greater risk of becoming dangerously cold or exhausted.

In calm conditions, the spray deck is largely used for the sake of convenience, but in rough water, a spray deck acts as the hatch cover for one of the biggest flotation compartments of your kayak—the cockpit. You need to choose a spray deck that can be

relied upon to stay on, even if a heavy wave were to crash on your deck. Of course, you also need to be able to be able to "pop" your spray deck and escape reliably.

The best spray decks for rough water feature an all-neoprene construction with a perimeter sewn shock cord specifically sized for a particular boat's coaming. These are the most reliable when it comes to resisting implosion from big waves, and are by far the driest. While spray decks can be made fully or in part out of

Your spray deck must fit your cockpit tightly enough so that it will not implode when loaded by breaking waves.

nylon (which vents better and costs less), they simply don't keep water out nearly as well. You'll also want to avoid adjustable one-size-fits-all decks that rely on a knotted shock cord to create a seal at the coaming; this approach yields unreliable results.

Helmet

For sea kayakers, the helmet is one of the most underused pieces of safety gear. If you plan on doing much paddling in rough water, then you should really invest in one. After all, if there is one part of your body that you should always protect, it's your head! This is particularly important if you're paddling in surf zones, or where there are objects in the water such as debris or ice. One of the great things about helmets is that they easily store on deck when you don't need them.

Helmets are generally manufactured out of plastic or composite materials like fiberglass, Kevlar® or carbon. Composite models are typically stiffer and will take a bigger hit, but cost more than plastic models.

As always, find a product that fits your own head well. The fit needs to be comfortable but secure. A helmet must be able to withstand a violent tumble in surf or current, and still stay firmly in place. A custom fit can easily be achieved by adding foam to the inside of a helmet, so take the time to adjust it to perfection.

A properly-fitted helmet is great, cheap insurance against possible head trauma—when you're wearing it. Do be aware though that if you are likely to need your helmet, put it on before leaving the beach. It may prove impossible to get a helmet off your deck and onto your head when you're dealing with raging surf or rushing current. When in doubt, wear your lid.

Dressing for Immersion – Warm and Cold Water

Deciding what to wear when paddling can feel challenging sometimes because you have to balance comfort with safety. This can feel especially tricky when the air is warm but the water is really cold. Conditions on the water are often incredibly changeable too. But for paddling in really rough conditions, the goal is clear:

always dress for immersion.

I will primarily address the strategy for paddling in cold water because this represents the greatest danger. Most swimmers get into serious trouble from the cold long before their swimming ability lets them down.

If you are preparing to launch into challenging conditions, or are likely to encounter them, you should be ready to get completely soaked. You may well get pelted by spray, lashed by waves and assaulted by wind. Be prepared to roll and even consider the possibility of an unplanned swim. Of course, the decision to dress for immersion must be made before leaving the beach, because getting changed in rough seas is no easy feat. When deciding specifically what to wear, keep in mind that it is by far preferable to be hot when paddling than to be cold, because it usually only takes a splashing of water to cool down. If a splash isn't enough, rolling will generally do the job. If you can't yet roll, then this is another good reason to learn.

Outer Layers

The outer layer and primary defense for any paddler is a waterproof paddling shell. A drytop with latex gaskets at the wrist and neck will keep you dry as long as you stay sealed in your boat. A full drysuit will keep you dry even in the event of a swim. Waterproof/breathable fabrics like Gore-Tex increase the comfort level of these garments by allowing vapor from your body to escape through the fabric, keeping you drier from perspiration. The ultimate in comfort and protection from cold water is a full Gore-Tex drysuit with built-in socks and a relief zipper. Built-in socks keep your feet warm and dry, and eliminate the need for tight latex gaskets around your ankles. The relief zipper is a terrifically convenient feature because it allows the calls of nature to be answered without removing the suit.

Any shell without gaskets at the wrists and neck will allow a substantial amount of water into the garment if you roll, and even more if you swim. Likewise, Velcro and neoprene closures alone

A wet exit in warm water.

When combined with a drytop, a neoprene farmer john wetsuit offers some valuable protection from cold water immersion. While a farmer john and drytop combo is a far second to a drysuit for overall warmth and comfort, the former option is a fraction of the cost.

A surfer's "steamer" wetsuit provides full coverage and very good insulation when in the water, but it is less comfortable for paddling. Because a steamer is designed to fit tightly, there is little water exchange even should a hole develop in the suit. For this reason, a full neoprene wetsuit does have the advantage of continuing to provide a good degree of insulation even if it is damaged and the suit begins to leak. This is not the case with a nylon drysuit which is wholly dependent on remaining intact to be completely waterproof and keep inner insulating layers dry. Some extreme paddlers who spend a lot of time in close proximity to sharp rocks that are likely to tear nylon drysuits therefore prefer to wear neoprene steamer suits.

Inner Layers

When considering insulating layers, be aware that not all fabrics are created equal. Cotton is one of the all-time worst materials to wear around cold water. It is not only very slow to dry (think

A drysuit or wetsuit offer different levels of protection against cold water conditions.

at the neck or wrists are no substitute for waterproof latex gaskets. It's great to be able to vent a paddling jacket, but don't expect it to provide much protection if you capsize.

Shells don't provide much warmth. They cut the wind effectively and keep you dry, but offer little insulation. The warmth of your system will be dictated by what you wear under your outer shell—and this is great, because it means that you can easily tailor your layering to reflect conditions.

Synthetic fabrics like polypropylene and fleece
are ideal insulating layers for paddling.

Pogies, neoprene gloves or mitts all do a good job of keeping hands warm. Without the circulation of warm blood to your hands and fingers, dexterity for even the easiest tasks is quickly lost. Try keying a VHF radio or untying a knot in a line with frozen digits and you'll know the importance of good hand protection.

A stout pair of wool socks and a good set of neoprene booties are the best solution that I have found for keeping feet warm. Neoprene socks in a pair of running or dedicated water shoes work really well too. Whatever your footwear, be sure that you have plenty of room to wiggle your toes. An overly tight fit will constrict blood vessels and reduce circulation, which will result in freezing cold feet.

The bottom line is that every day you spend on the water will likely present different weather and temperatures. You'll need to assess the conditions, and then dress accordingly. If in doubt, wear an extra layer, because you're always better off being too warm than too cold. Remember that your kayak also has a ton of space for extra clothing, so don't be shy about bringing it along on day trips and short outings. Ultimately though, if you are paddling in rough conditions, you will not have the option of making major wardrobe changes until you land again. Dry warm fleece packed in your day hatch won't keep you warm while you're in the water; it will only help once you're wearing it. So when it's rough or likely to be, dress for immersion.

about how your heavy cotton jeans are always the last thing to be done in the drier) but it generates a tremendous amount of convection cooling—so cotton will actually rob heat from your body, rather than keep it warm. Of course, this same attribute can be used to good advantage if you are paddling in really hot conditions in warm water and need to cool yourself.

Choose fabrics that deal with moisture well and dry quickly. Polyester synthetics like fleece and polypropylene work extremely well and dry quickly. There is also a new generation of merino wool garments that provide excellent warmth and comfort, although drying times are a little longer than for synthetics.

Accessories

Protecting your head, hands and feet is important too. A warm hat or skullcap and helmet will help retain precious body heat.

Safety Gear

There are a number of items that should come along every time you paddle, especially when heading into more demanding conditions. They can easily be carried on every excursion, and their inclusion in your kit should become part of your normal pre-trip packing routine.

Safety gear that should accompany every rough water kayak trip includes:

- Spare paddle
- coastguard-approved PFD (should include a whistle)

The combination of a deck-mounted compass and a waterproof chart-case is best for on-water kayak navigation.

- Towline
- Bilge pump
- Extra warm clothing and overnight emergency bag (warm waterproof clothing, tarp/shelter, space blanket, headlamp, knife, fire starter and food like energy bars, etc.)
- Drinking water and snacks
- Chart and compass where applicable
- Marine radio and/or cell phone where applicable

- Signaling devices (flares, mirror, strobe, smoke canister)
- First aid kit

Signaling Devices

Signaling devices can be very useful pieces of safety equipment. Sometimes they may be the only way to communicate that you need help. But remember that flares and smoke canisters are only deployed after something has gone terribly wrong and you find

A waterproof VHF radio provides easy access to weather forecasts and communication with other boaters and the coastguard.

Strobes work well at night or in any other low-light situation. They can be attached to the shoulder strap of your PFD, but like flares, should only be activated on the water in true emergency situations, because a strobe represents a mayday signal. They depend on batteries, so always make sure that the units are fully charged before heading out, or bring extra batteries.

Whistles or horns are also good for getting people's attention. A simple plastic whistle will allow you to make far more noise, far longer, and with much less effort than yelling ever could. Attach a whistle to your PFD with a short lanyard so you can easily blow into it without fear of losing it.

VHF radios provide another powerful means of signaling for help, because they reach other boats in the area as well as the coastguard. You can even use a VHF radio to make a phone call through a marine operator—but perhaps most importantly, you can access marine weather forecasts easily. There is an operating protocol for these radios which is designed to reduce channel overcrowding and to keep certain channels open to distress calls. Make sure that if you are carrying a VHF radio that you are trained in how to use them properly. Because VHF radios rely on batteries, exercise care to limit power consumption, especially when broadcasting, which consumes the most power. Opt for a waterproof handheld VHF. In a kayak, a radio that stops working once it's wet (and it will get wet) is of little value.

Cell phones can also come in handy, although you never know when you'll be out of range with them. As with all electronics, batteries and susceptibility to death by moisture are big limiting factors. Electronics are useful tools, but over-dependence on gear that fails easily in the field is unwise.

Emergency Bag

For day-trips, it's really easy to throw together an emergency "overnight bag". A 5 gallon (20 liter) drybag of gear can make such a huge difference that I can't understand why more paddlers don't take the time to assemble one.

yourself in a true emergency situation. Your goal should be to play safe and never have cause to launch a flare.

Flares do work well on overcast days and especially at night. Carry at least three and ensure that they are within the expiration date stamped on their sides. In very high winds, (a time when emergency situations could feasibly develop), flares do not hang in the sky for very long at all. They rise up, are snatched by the wind and whipped into the sea. Multiple flares greatly increase the chance of successfully signaling a passing vessel.

Smoke canisters are effective during daylight, although they're not great on windy days, because wind will dissipate the smoke quickly.

The following take up little space and will make a huge difference should you need to do an unplanned bivouac: extra clothing to help keep you warm and dry, a tarp, space blanket (do not expect miracles from these, they only serve to cut the wind and little else), waterproof headlamp, knife, fire starter and food like energy bars. Even a few hours spent waiting out fog or surf can be absolutely miserable if you are cold and wet. You don't need to bring so much stuff that you can spend a night out in perfect luxury and comfort, but you should be equipped to spend a night without it being an absolutely punishing ordeal.

Get in the habit of stuffing an overnight bag in your boat. Its inclusion will also give you greater latitude when making judgment calls. Obviously, the nature of your trip and its specific risks will dictate exactly what you bring. For coastal routes in populated areas where there are many good landing options, you are unlikely to get caught out and will likely pack a more minimalist bag. However, if you are contemplating something like a difficult crossing to a distant island that is subject to heavy fog and high winds, you might just opt to throw your tent, sleeping bag and stove in with the basic overnight bag.

A thermos of piping hot tea, chicken soup or hot chocolate is also a favorite with many paddlers. Being able to quickly access a big mug of steaming liquid is a great way to warm a cold body, and does wonders for morale as well.

Be sure to include a basic first aid kit too.

Other Personal Gear

There are a number of other pieces of gear that can help make your sea kayaking adventures more comfortable and safer.

Hydration packs are an unobtrusive and efficient way for a paddler to stay hydrated. Because it is so easy to drink frequently, and there is no need to pop the spray deck to access a bottle, kayakers can sip as much water as they want. With the drinking tube in place, there isn't any need to miss a stroke.

Staying hydrated will make a huge difference to how good

A hydration bladder is a great addition, allowing a paddler to drink freely without the need to open the spray deck or fumble with a bottle.

you'll feel over the day, and help you recover from your exertions. You'll sleep better and be fresher for the next day's challenges. Dehydration will rob you of energy and make you sick. Being overheated and dehydrated is an invitation to motion sickness. Vomiting induced by motion sickness will in turn cause even greater dehydration.

Sun protection is also a major concern. Sun block is a good idea even on overcast days, as is a wide-brimmed hat and sunglasses.

Snacks in the form of energy bars and such can be easily stashed in PFD pockets or paddling tops. Any arrangement that allows access to food without the need to pop the spray deck is a good idea. Remember that when it's rough, it may be impossible to do anything other than actively paddle.

Remember that you are the motor for your watercraft, so you need to make sure that everything is running smoothly. Your body needs fuel and water to run efficiently—and you need to ensure that you are adequately protected against the elements. If your body fails, the motor stalls, and you will be in serious trouble.

2

MECHANICS & STROKES

THE THREE GOLDEN RULES STAYING UPRIGHT EDGING BRACES
PROPELLING STROKES TURNING STROKES SCULLING

This book assumes a solid grasp of standard paddling technique. Rather than breaking each stroke and technique into its base components, we will concentrate on specific elements of established skills that are key to success in rough conditions. Consequently, we will spend little time outlining the individual elements of strokes in favor of describing how to best execute them in real world, rough water conditions.

THE THREE GOLDEN RULES

Use Co-operative Division of the Body

Maintain the Power Position

Rotate Your Torso

The "Three Golden Rules" are a set of rules that should be applied regardless of the type of sea kayaking that you intend to do. Adhering to these three basic concepts will give you a great advantage when paddling in tougher conditions by giving you good mechanics—so that you are always in a strong, supple position. Following these rules will allow you to paddle smoothly with power, and protect your shoulders from injury too.

#1 Use Co-operative Division of the Body

The co-operative division of the body refers to the notion of letting your upper and lower body work co-operatively yet independently from each other. For example, your upper body may be actively driving your kayak forward, while your lower body is holding your boat on edge. Similarly, your boat may rock from edge to edge in rough water while your upper body stays

The upper and lower body work co-operatively yet independently from each other.

Like many strokes, a stern rudder requires aggressive torso rotation and the arms kept in the power position.

upright. This co-operative division of work is essential to edging, bracing, rolling and all other advanced paddling techniques.

#2 Maintain the Power Position

Sea kayaking in rough conditions exposes a paddler to the powerful forces of moving water, and unfortunately injuries can occur. The most common injuries are relatively minor ones like blisters or tendonitis, but shoulder dislocation is a serious injury that is unfortunately all too common. One of the best ways to prevent shoulder injury is to maintain the "power position" with your arms.

The power position simply involves keeping your hands in front of your body. Another way to think of it is that your arms,

chest and paddle form a box when you hold your paddle in front of you, and you should maintain this box when taking any type of stroke. This doesn't mean that you can't reach to the back of your boat to take a stroke. But it does mean that in order to do so, you'll need to rotate your whole upper body so that your hands stay in front of you. This act of rotating the upper body is fittingly referred to as torso rotation. Not only does this keep your shoulders safe, but it lets you harness the most power for your strokes, which is why it's our Third Golden Rule!

#3 Rotate Your Torso

Your paddle strokes should use much more than just your arm and shoulder muscles. You need to use the power of your whole upper body. Torso rotation is the way to get your front and side stomach muscles involved with your strokes. With good rotation, you should be working your latissimus dorsi muscles, or "lats", too. Using these larger muscles will let you paddle harder, faster, and for longer.

STAYING UPRIGHT

When considering rough water paddling technique, there is always much talk of bracing, surfing and rolling. But long before any of those skills are examined, attention should be focused on the fundamental element of flexing from the waist, and on staying supple and "fluid" above the boat.

Much of the time, the key to staying upright in rough conditions is staying relaxed and letting your boat "go with the flow" while your upper body remains centered and balanced over your kayak. To do this, your waist needs to operate like a universal joint, allowing the kayak to incline freely in all directions.

Picture paddling over a small on-coming wave. The bow will climb the face of the wave, crest it and then carry on down the far

side. The boat's angle along its length changes from an upward tilt to a downward one. Adjusting to this change in boat angle is very natural. The paddler simply leans forward or backward from the waist and hips, effectively keeping the upper body in a neutral position, while the kayak rides over the wave. The paddler's head stays over the centerline of the kayak and therefore no loss of stability is experienced.

We are naturally good at leaning forward or back in a kayak, but flexing edge to edge usually feels counter-intuitive. If the paddler stays rigid at the waist when the boat moves edge to edge, the mass of the upper body and head will lean out over the centerline and throw the paddler off balance. The key is to stay supple and keep your head over the centerline.

Of course, staying relaxed is easier said than done. It helps to focus on a deep, comfortable breathing rhythm. Match that to the rhythm of your strokes and feel the calm that results.

Remaining relaxed in your kayak will help to keep you flexible and limber, allowing the kayak to pitch, roll side to side, and move fore and aft—while you stay centered. If you do not flex from the waist, every little wave or splash will cause you to bobble or throw you completely off balance.

EDGING

Tilting your kayak on edge is an essential skill for paddling in rough water, tight places, breaking waves or swift currents. It allows you to deal with waves and current and to turn your kayak more efficiently.

Edging is accomplished by dropping one knee and raising the other. Think in terms of loading one butt cheek or the other, while keeping your upper body and head over the kayak. With practice, it will become easy to quickly edge your boat to either side, maintain it held on edge, or smoothly transition from one edge to the other.

When tilting your boat on edge, remember to keep your hips

The kayak is held on edge by the lower body, while the upper body is balanced over the boat.

Edging is generally done for two fundamental reasons:
- To turn your kayak faster.
- To manage waves and current.

Edging to Turn

To turn your kayak faster, you can edge your boat to the inside or the outside of the turn (depending on what stroke you are doing). Edging your boat either way will yield a tighter turning radius and increase maneuverability. The reason why this works is that placing a kayak on edge drastically changes the boat's "footprint".

A kayak's footprint is the shape that its hull makes in the water. Imagine standing on the bottom of the sea, looking up at a kayak floating on the surface. As the boat is forced on edge, the shape that its hull makes in the water changes. The overall waterline,

loose and your weight balanced over your kayak. Now shift your weight slightly over to one butt cheek and lift the opposite knee. You should feel your whole rib cage shifting over to that side of your kayak. Your stomach and side muscles will be working to keep your body upright, while your legs hold a steady tilt on your boat. In particular, your top knee will be pulling upward on its thigh hook.

Make no mistake, holding your kayak on edge is a skill that takes plenty of practice. Your ultimate goal is to be able to hold your boat on edge and still take effective strokes. One of the best ways to practice this is to try to hold your boat on edge as you paddle forward.

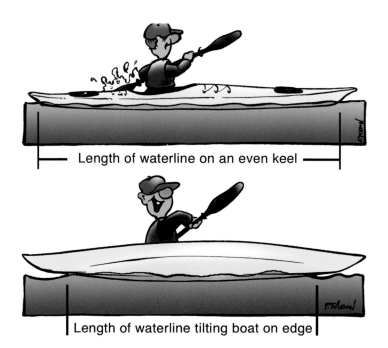

Length of waterline on an even keel

Length of waterline tilting boat on edge

or length of the boat that is immersed, will shorten. The kayak, when pushed onto its edge or seam line, also has more rocker. The keel at the stern will also load, or catch, far less water. All of these factors help the boat turn much faster.

Edging to Manage Waves and Current

When paddling in current or waves, it is often necessary to aggressively edge the kayak one way to avoid accidentally loading or catching the other edge of your boat, which would flip you upside down.

In current, water will swiftly flow under the hull of your kayak. When the current is traveling at any angle other than parallel to your kayak, water will have a tendency to load on the upstream side of your boat. Edging downstream will keep your upstream edge out of the water and prevent it from loading. Failure to edge downstream will allow water to load on the upstream side, catch that edge, and flip you over with surprising speed.

In breaking waves, a kayak will be pushed across the surface of the water by the power of the waves. In this case, you must lean away from the direction that the kayak is skimming across the water. Failure to do so will engage the leading edge of the boat and flip it. To stay upright and in control, expose the bottom of your boat to the oncoming water by leaning your boat into the wave. In other words, edge it on the side that the wave is approaching your boat. (If you are familiar with whitewater paddling, this is similar in concept to how, in whitewater, you maintain control by edging on the upstream side of your boat.)

BRACES

A brace is used to recover when you've been thrown off balance. There are two forms of braces, and both involve reaching out to the side of your kayak with your paddle and slapping the water with one blade. The only major difference between the low and the high brace is the position of your paddle as you slap the water. For both, the slap provides the momentary support needed for your body to upright your kayak. This is critical to understand. The paddle just provides momentary support—your body is responsible for righting the boat. Let's take a quick look at how it does this.

As you flip, the only way to right the kayak is by pulling up with the knee that is going underwater. The only way to pull up with this knee is to drop your head towards the water in the direction that you're flipping. I know this sounds counter-intuitive—which is precisely why it's difficult to develop the habit when you're learning—but it's absolutely essential. If you lift your head up, you'll inadvertently pull on your top knee, which simply flips you even more quickly.

By dropping your head, you lower your center of gravity, and allow your lower knee to pull up and roll the kayak upright.

A good way to encourage your head to drop towards the water is to watch your slapping blade as you brace. It's hard to lift your head if you're looking downward.

Low Brace

The low brace is the ideal recovery technique because you must keep your paddle low, which helps prevent shoulder injuries. It's also the quickest brace to do, so it's great in emergency situations.

Sitting upright, roll the paddle under your elbows so that your forearms are almost vertical, almost as though you were going to do a push-up. Reach out to 90 degrees so that one hand is at your belly button and the other is out over the water. Edging the boat in the direction that you brace, slap the water, drop your head in that direction and pull up with your lower knee to level off the kayak. Make sure that your paddle hits the water flat, parallel to the surface, which will give you the most powerful support. To finish the brace, pull your paddle forward and inward, and roll your knuckles upward to clear the blade from the water.

| Reach out with the paddle in a push-up position. | Smack the water with the back of the blade. | Right the kayak by dropping your head and lifting the lower knee. | Roll your knuckles forward and up to clear the paddle from the water. |

The low brace is really effective and lightning-quick. In rough conditions, the low brace can be blended with just about any other stroke for quick momentary support can keep you connected with the water's movement. I often use the low brace more as a "point of contact" with the water, than as a truly loaded emergency brace. For example, whenever I feel that I may be at risk of losing stability, I'll use a quick low brace to keep contact with the surface and lock me upright.

Regardless of what stroke I am performing, every time that my paddle blade contacts the water, I have the chance to load the blade and generate support. Depending on how my blade, boat, and body are oriented, I can create lift and support from the paddle face.

For example, if I'm waiting for a paddling partner to catch up, I may be in bouncy water, looking back over my shoulder. Simply laying my paddle out to the side in a relaxed low brace position gives me a lot of stability, and this way the brace is already queued up and ready to go if I do need to actually use it. More importantly, it makes me feel far more connected to the water.

A solid low brace can almost feel like training wheels on your kayak when things get unexpectedly wobbly—only instead of being a permanent fixture, these training wheels take a millisecond to install, and are gone again when you're ready to edge.

The only time that you should give way from the low brace to a high brace is when your boat is on such a steep angle that you run out of room to lift the blade higher. This will happen with large foam piles or waves in surf, or when you have fallen so far over that the boat is on an extreme angle.

High Brace

The high brace is definitely the most powerful of the recovery techniques. A good paddler can even use the high brace to recover when their boat is almost completely upside down!

The high brace follows the same rules as the low brace, only this time you'll be using your paddle in a "chin-up" position, instead of the "push-up" position, and you'll be using the power face instead of the backside of the blades. While sitting up straight, keep your elbows low, and roll your paddle up until your forearms are almost vertical.

Tilt your boat and combine the head drop and knee pull up with your motions. This means that as you slap the water, you'll drop your head towards the water and pull up with your lowest knee to right the kayak. Remember that looking at your active blade is a good habit to get into because it helps keep your head down.

The only problem with the high brace is that it's easy to rely on it too heavily and this puts you at higher risk of injuring your shoulders. The first thing to keep in mind is that despite its name,

1	2	3	4
Reach out with the paddle in a chin-up position.	Smack the water with the power-face of the blade.	Right the kayak by dropping your head and lifting the lower knee.	The head is the last thing to come up!

you need to keep your paddle and your hands low and in front of your body. Shoulder dislocation is a common injury for paddlers, so maintain a power position and avoid desperate "Hail Mary" high braces.

In large breaking waves and foam piles, or when recovering from extreme leans and near capsizes, the high brace is the best tool to use. Just remember that for even the biggest high braces, you've got to keep your hands low to keep your shoulders safe.

SAFETY

Avoid the dreaded "downstream brace". When side-surfing a foam pile or a powerful wave, it is far safer to roll than attempt a "downstream brace". In a side-surf position, your kayak will be edged toward the wave or foam pile. Water will be racing past the leading edge of your kayak, opposite the edge angled into the foam. If you catch that leading edge of the kayak in the oncoming water, your kayak will instantly be flipped violently. Vainly sticking a "Hail Mary" high brace out on the downstream side will not only fail to keep you upright, but it is also an almost guaranteed recipe for injury or dislocation of the shoulder joint. If you suddenly "power flip", just go with it, tucking into a nice defensive roll setup position. Roll up on the foam pile side and continue to play.

PROPELLING STROKES

Forward Stroke

An efficient and powerful forward stroke is an absolute must for any sea kayaker. Because so much of our time is spent paddling forward, it's essential to get the most out of each and every paddle stroke.

The key to a powerful forward stroke is to carefully work on each component (catch, rotation, and exit), and be sure to really emphasize torso rotation. Without involving the big powerful muscles of the torso, you'll never harness your full potential to drive a kayak forward.

In moving water, sometimes all that is needed is a brief spurt of power, consisting of only a few explosive strokes. It may be to blast through a strong rip current, catch a surf ride on a wave, or to sprint out through an opening in surf. For brief sprints, adopting a very vertical paddle stroke is most effective. Shorten your stroke and increase the cadence, while still employing full

The ability to paddle forward aggressively with the boat on edge is a prerequisite for confident navigation through strong current.

torso rotation for power. Developing a really strong three-to-six-stroke sprint will come in very handy for both catching waves and punching through them. A strong, short-burst sprint is often the best tool for avoiding nasty thrashings in surf and current.

Forward Paddling on Edge

It's not enough to have a powerful and efficient forward stroke, you'll also want to develop the ability to paddle aggressively with your kayak held on edge.

Edging your kayak will cause it to turn away from the direction that you're tilting your boat. The more you tilt your kayak, the more aggressively your kayak will turn. Learning to steer your boat with edging is a necessary skill, especially to paddle with confidence in rough water, where edging is essential for staying upright when meeting strong currents or waves. It will also let you make small corrections while paddling forward without losing speed.

A great drill for improving balance and edge control is to paddle forward in a straight line while holding your kayak on edge. Work on one edge, and then switch from one to the other after about ten strokes. Practice alternating from edge to edge until it becomes smooth and controlled.

Practice paddling forward on edge on both sides.

NOTE

In a rescue situation, it's often tempting to spin your kayak around in order to rescue a capsized kayaker behind you. These complicated maneuvers are inefficient and time-consuming, especially in rough water. Instead of turning your boat around, use three or four well-placed back strokes. You'll be at the swimmer's side in a fraction of the time.

TURNING STROKES

Sweep Stroke

The sweep stroke is without a doubt the best stroke for turning your kayak, and as you know by now, tilting your kayak aggressively into your forward or reverse sweep stroke makes it most effective. To turn your kayak in rough water, the sweep stroke remains your best choice, although there are a couple of things to consider.

Traditionally it is taught that you should follow your sweeping blade with your eyes. The reason for this is that it promotes torso rotation and helps get your whole body into the stroke. Although this does make great sense in most situations, in rough conditions like rock gardens or surf, it's extremely important to keep your eyes on where you're going. This means that you will often want to lead your turns with your head instead of watching your paddle blade throughout the stroke. The problem with leading with your head is that it doesn't promote torso rotation, so it's easy to get lazy and not fully finish the stroke. Practice good full sweeps, being sure to finish the stroke to maximize turning potential, while still keeping your eyes on where you're heading.

In really large, rough seas, or extremely confused waters, the best course of action will be to keep your boat on an even keel, or flat to the water. You'll definitely want to edge your kayak to deal

Back Stroke

Although you won't use the back stroke all that often, it can be really useful at times, especially when you're paddling in surf or current or making a rescue.

In a lot of ways, the back stroke is fairly intuitive, but steering while going backwards definitely isn't. The only way to get comfortable steering while moving backwards is by practicing.

When trying to punch through big surf, it is not at all unusual to get surfed backwards after failing to make it over a wave. In this situation, lack of familiarity with paddling backwards almost always leads to a violent capsize. With some practice and experience, the back stroke will give you far greater control in a back-surf and greatly increase your chances of not only staying upright, but of smoothly navigating big surf without mishap.

When performing a forward sweep with your boat on edge, torso rotation provides the power, while a climbing angle on the blade offers support.

with waves or current in this setting, but edging the kayak for a sweep stroke is not worth the risk of being thrown off balance by dynamic conditions. With the boat on an even keel, the kayak will turn far more slowly, but you can offset this by timing a sweep to coincide with your kayak cresting a wave. At the crest of a wave, the bow and all-important stern section of the keel (which greatly influences the tracking of the boat) will be free of the water, and consequently the kayak will rotate far more readily.

Bracing Lean Turns

A bracing lean turn is a moving turn done with forward speed. The paddler rolls their kayak onto its edge and uses the support of a paddle blade on the inside of the turn. The paddle helps turn the kayak, but supports the edging of the boat, which is what makes these turns so effective. Bracing lean turns can be done on either a low or high brace.

A key element to both the high brace and low brace lean turn is the need for a climbing angle on the supporting blade. A climbing angle means that the leading edge of your paddle blade is higher than the trailing edge. This makes your paddle want to stay on the surface and lets you get support from it without having it sink.

Both turns start with forward speed and are initiated with a forward sweep stroke. If you want to turn to the right, you'll use a forward sweep stroke on the left.

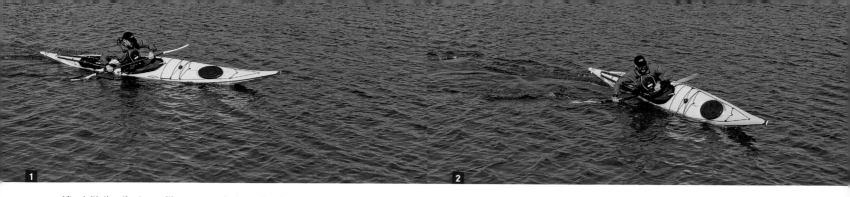

After initiating the turn with a sweep, plant your low brace near the stern with a climbing angle on the blade.	Weight the paddle and roll your kayak up on edge.

Low Brace Lean Turn

For the low brace turn, as soon as you've initiated the turn with the sweep on the left, you'll rotate your upper body to take a reverse sweep on the right, and then lean your body and tilt your boat into the stroke. The more aggressively you'd like to turn, the more aggressively you'll put your kayak on edge. Remember that your paddle needs to sweep out to the side of your kayak with a climbing angle on the blade, so that it provides both support and turning power. You should be able to really "hang" on the low brace through a good portion of the turn. As your boat reaches the end of its turn, your blade should have swept forward to a point directly out to the side from your hip. It's important to realize that as your kayak slows down, the amount of support you'll get from your brace drops considerably, so you'll want to flatten out your kayak towards the end of the turn.

The low brace lean turn places the shoulders in a really strong position, keeping them safe from injury, and works really well in any situation where you want quick turning ability and don't mind losing your forward speed. It's a great way to enter and exit eddies, carve off of small waves or get your boat turned around in the surf zone, all of which we'll look at more closely in Chapter 4.

After initiating the turn with a sweep, plant your high brace with wrists cocked back to create a climbing angle on the blade.	Keeping the arm low and close to the body, weight the blade and roll the kayak on edge.

As the turn progresses and the boat decelerates, sweep the low brace out to the side and forward.

Level off the kayak at the end of the turn and reach forward for your next stroke.

High Brace Lean Turn

The high brace lean turn is virtually the same as the low brace lean turn, only you'll be using a high brace for support, and you won't use the same reverse sweep motions. Instead, after initiating the turn with a forward sweep on the opposite side, you'll plant your high brace out to the side of your kayak, just behind your hip, with a climbing angle on the power face of the blade. Make sure that you keep your upper hand quite low, with the elbow tucked into the body to keep your shoulders safe. As before, the climbing angle on your paddle is achieved by cocking your wrists back. This allows you to get steady support from your blade as your boat travels forward and also helps turn your kayak. Once the turn is complete, and you've leveled out your boat tilt, you can transition smoothly from the high brace to a forward stroke by slicing your blade forward.

Remember that the support you get from either the low and high brace comes from your motion relative to the water. This means that as you slow down through the turn, you'll get less support from the brace and will need to level off your kayak or be prepared to balance without support.

Much of the time I prefer the low brace lean turn to the high

As the boat decelerates sweep your high brace forward and level off the kayak.

The high brace lean turn leaves you in a great position for a powerful forward stroke.

1	2	3	4
With the kayak edged away from the stroke, rotate your torso toward the paddle and plant your blade.	Cock your wrists back to open the angle of your blade so that the power face catches water.	Draw your blade to your toes in a sweeping arc to finish the stroke.	Level out the kayak and finish with a forward stroke to keep your forward momentum.

brace version, except sometimes when I'm peeling into or out of eddies, and sometimes coming off of waves. A high brace lean turn allows you to open the face of the blade more and grab more water for more aggressive, zippy turns, which means that you are actually blending a bow rudder with a high brace. The two strokes share similar body and blade positions.

Bow Draw

The bow draw is a very efficient and elegant solution for making minor course corrections and avoiding obstacles when traveling forward. A bow draw is also a great stroke for drawing yourself away from rocks when waves or current threaten to push you sideways. If you're playing among rocks, shooting the gap between boulders, or charging a surge channel, a bow draw combined with a little forward momentum can give you the last-second fine-tuning required to ensure that you nail your line and "thread the needle" successfully.

To do a bow draw, plant your paddle in front of your body, about a foot or two out to the side by your knee. Your blade should be angled so that the power face of your paddle catches water. Draw the blade to your toes in a sweeping arc so that it ends in a perfect position for a forward stroke. To get the most turning power from your bow draw, initiate the turn with a sweep stroke on the opposite side of your bow draw and then plant your paddle further out to the side of your kayak than you otherwise might, with your wrists cocked back to catch lots of water. You can also help your turn by initiating it at the peak of a wave, and/or by tilting your boat away from your draw. This stroke can generate a lot of force and so it is important to keep your body safe by keeping your arms close to the body and in the power position. This means planting your bow draw with your upper body aggressively rotated towards it. Full rotation of your torso will place your lower wrist in a far stronger, straighter position and will cause less strain on the joint. If your wrist is excessively cocked back, rotate more to the side of the stroke. Check your arm positions too: your upper arm should reach across the forehead to place the paddle shaft in the water in a very upright position. The lower arm should be fairly close to the body to keep your shoulder safe.

Start playing with bow strokes on flat water. Once you get comfortable with how they feel and you develop a good sense of how effectively they can move your bow, these strokes will naturally start to find their way into your paddling stroke repertoire.

SCULLING

While all other strokes involve catch and release points, sculling is a technique that lets you get steady support from your paddle blade. We're going to take a quick look at the sculling draw and the sculling brace, although sculling has applications beyond these strokes. The paddle dexterity that sculling teaches is a clear benefit when paddling in rough conditions and you have to react to the many forces acting upon you and your kayak.

Sculling Brace

The sculling brace is an advanced bracing technique that lets you get steady support from your paddle blade. The key is to keep your paddle moving back and forth, parallel to your kayak, and to keep your blade on a climbing angle. A climbing angle means that the leading edge of your paddle blade is higher than the trailing edge. This makes your paddle want to climb to the surface and lets you get support from it without it sinking. Cock your wrists back as you push forward on your paddle, and curl your wrists forward as you pull back on your paddle. With alternating, quick and powerful strokes like this, you can get steady support from your paddle blade. Remember, as always, to keep your arms low and your shoulders safe.

Sculling Draw

The sculling draw stroke is the most effective means of moving your kayak laterally. Not only is this helpful for pulling up beside a dock, but it is a key stroke in almost every rescue scenario. A sculling draw stroke is also an incredibly useful tool for staying in one place and not moving sideways. For example, when navigating surge channels or rock gardens, one of the biggest challenges is resisting the action of current or waves, which may be trying to sweep you sideways and off line. A strong sculling

For the sculling draw, keep the paddle as vertical as possible and rotate your torso aggressively to face the paddle.

Maintain constant pressure on your sculling blade by cocking your wrists back slightly as you push your paddle forward, and then rolling your wrists forward as you pull your paddle backward.

The top hand acts like a pivot while the stroke is driven by torso rotation.

stroke is absolutely essential to good boat control, and a stroke that is all too often neglected by sea kayakers.

The sculling draw is a much more powerful draw than the traditional T-stroke, although it is set up in the same way. Plant your blade completely in the water, out at a 90 degree angle from your hip. Rotate your head and upper body aggressively to face your paddle's power-face, which is parallel to the centerline of your boat. Position your top hand so that it's pushed across your boat, placing your paddle shaft in as vertical a position as possible. Instead of pulling directly into your hip, you'll use the same sculling motion that we just looked at for the sculling brace, only you'll be doing it on the vertical plane. The key is keeping your paddle blade moving along a short path forward and backward about a foot or two away to the side of your kayak, with a blade angle that opens your power face to the oncoming water and pulls your paddle away from your kayak. This means that you'll cock your wrists slightly back to open your power face as you slice your blade forward, and then make a quick transition and curl your wrists forward as you slice your blade backward.

Don't forget that just like for any other stroke, the power for your sculling draw comes from your torso rotation. This is why it's so important that you turn your body aggressively into the stroke. The forward and backward movement of your paddle can then be driven by your torso rotation, and your arms will stay in a relatively fixed position.

The sculling draw should be a very active component in your toolbox of strokes. It will allow you to control what your boat does laterally, keep you on line for maneuvering in tight spots where current or waves are acting upon your kayak, and help to promote an awareness of blade angle and feathering in the water.

Stern Rudder

A stern rudder is the most powerful means of making small corrections to your course without slowing your kayak's forward momentum too much. Most notably, it will help you stay on

The stern pry provides the best control for surfing.

track when paddling in wind and waves. It's also the stroke that you'll use to control your kayak while surfing waves, which we'll discuss in more detail in the *Surfing* section of Chapter 4.

There are two forms of the stern rudder. There's the stern pry, and the stern draw. Both of these strokes start from the same position, with your paddle planted firmly in the water behind your body, parallel to your kayak. To do this, and still keep your hands in front of your body in the power position, you'll need to use some aggressive torso rotation, which means turning your whole upper body towards your rudder. Hold your front hand comfortably in front of your chest. From this position, you can either push away with the backside of your paddle blade, which is called the stern pry, or you can draw water towards your stern with your power face, which is called the stern draw. The stern pry is by far the more powerful of the two strokes, and the one that you'll use most of the time.

When surfing waves, there is always potential for dynamic capsizes, so always be sure to rotate your upper body aggressively to plant your rudder, because this allows you to maintain your power position and prevent shoulder injury. It's also important that you completely submerge your rudder as far back as is comfortable, with the paddle parallel to the kayak. This will provide your stroke with the most power while minimizing any braking effect.

Blending Strokes

Throughout this book, we have stressed the concept of smoothly transitioning from one stroke to another. This is sometimes achieved without the paddle even breaking the surface of the water. By adjusting paddle angle and feathering the blade through the water, the power face can be relocated and loaded on a different angle or plane, in order to generate lift in a different direction. It's this flowing transition from one stroke to the next that provides a paddler with constant, steady control of the kayak. It's also what separates a competent paddler from a really good one.

Linking strokes requires that you have a good feel for the angle of your blade in the water, and the paddle dexterity to make small adjustments to keep your movements smooth and efficient. Developing this type of control will go a long way towards building your confidence on the water, and making you a more dynamic paddler with improved boat control.

3

ROUGH WATER SAFETY

THE FUNDAMENTALS ROUGH WATER RESCUES AIDED RE-ENTRY RESCUES

THE FUNDAMENTALS

Caring for Your Kayak and Gear

An equipment failure in rough seas can have a devastating effect, so it is important that you not only choose quality gear, but that you maintain your gear.

With any kayak, there are some common potential-failure areas to keep an eye on. Rudders, rudder-cables and hardware can all be weak points. For most rudder-equipped boats, if a rudder-cable snaps, the rudder will flop to one side and be impossible to use. Even more importantly, the foot pedal inside the boat will slide forward becoming useless to brace against. The loss of a pedal will seriously compromise your fit in the boat and your ability to grip the kayak. Always pay close attention to the condition of rudder cables, and associated hardware. Also routinely check that the rudder itself is securely mounted to the boat and hasn't sustained any damage in transport or while afloat.

Skegs can be problematic too. Skeg boxes often leak, although a little marine sealant will usually solve that problem. Pebbles and grit can also jam skegs. If this happens, resist the urge to tug on the slider, because this will only kink the wire or cable. Some paddlers opt to drill a small hole in their skeg blade, and then attach a short loop (2-3" or about 10 cm) of fishing line to it. This provides a convenient handle with minimal drag. By reaching under the boat, and gripping the loop, a paddling partner can usually free the skeg and clear it of debris, without needing to head back to shore. One of the nice things about skegs is that even if they get damaged to the point that they are inoperable, it won't compromise your fit in the kayak. Skeg-equipped boats have foot pedals that are bolted directly to the hull and so are unaffected by damage to the skeg.

Seats are also subject to a lot of wear and tear. Seat-backs and back-bands can loosen or fail, so make sure that you routinely inspect the cockpit area for any potential weak spots and make repairs as needed.

Do your homework and always show up to paddle with your kayak and gear in full working order. If you know that you have a minor mechanical problem that could potentially affect your performance, deal with it before it becomes an issue at sea.

Even with the best maintenance, equipment can still fail unexpectedly, so carry a small repair kit for emergency work in the field. Include any extra hardware that you think might prove useful, and the tools necessary to install it. Duct tape is an absolute essential, invaluable for repairing almost anything, including patching holes punched in boats. Just be sure to dry surfaces thoroughly, or even duct tape won't stick! A tube of marine sealant can be extremely useful too, and some paddlers also carry a basic composite repair kit consisting of fiberglass cloth, resin and catalyst.

Even seemingly minor equipment failures can become epic

YOU NEED A TRAILER

F. Mason

Polyethylene kayaks are almost indestructible and therefore ideal for abusive applications like seal launches.

catastrophes in the wrong conditions, particularly when several unexpected problems occur at once and the troubles start to pile up. It's alarming how minor snags have a tendency to compound, and before you know it, that little mishap that was going to be so simple to deal with is about to test you to your limits. Things can go quickly out of control when you are challenging yourself in tougher conditions. You can't completely prevent problems from popping up now and again, but you can certainly strive to minimize the frequency with which they occur, and be prepared to handle them properly when they do.

Group Dynamics and Leadership

When paddling with a group in rough water, one of the greatest issues is communication—both in the sense of simply being able to pass information back and forth while paddling, but also in terms of establishing clear protocols for decision-making and goal-setting, both before, and after hitting the water.

It's important for everyone in a group to understand what role they will play, the other paddlers' abilities and expectations, and finally to honestly communicate one's own ideas and limitations. A lot of it is really simple. By establishing things like skill levels within the group, conditioning and comfort zones, a lot of grief can be avoided. Similarly, who will lead, what route is to be taken, bail-out options, and even what rescue technique is most likely to be used, all need to be discussed and clearly understood. By having established procedures in place, valuable time will be saved, and confusion, frustration, and disappointment avoided.

Leadership doesn't necessarily involve always taking the lead at the front of the herd, but it does mean fostering a clear and

A tight group formation makes communication far easier and drastically reduces rescue time should a paddler require assistance.

transparent exchange of information within the group. The idea is to achieve a commonly held and clearly articulated goal or outcome. It might be to circumnavigate an island, or "go and play in that rip over there". But whatever the goal, it is important that the group fully understands the mission, individual roles on the water and off, and that all group members be clear and comfortable with the group's decision.

Leadership can also mean acting decisively when a quick decision is needed. There is no need to call an on-water meeting to ratify a plan for towing a swimmer away from a rocky shore where he's in danger of being pummeled by waves. In that case, it is best to get on with the rescue after a quick and assertive: "I'm going after him". The rest of the group should stand by, but be ready to assist in any way possible.

However you travel as a group, remember that your group is only as strong as its weakest link, and that all members of the group are equally entitled to feeling safe and having fun while afloat.

Risk Assessment

Risk is an inherent part of paddling in challenging conditions. The goal is not to avoid all risk all the time, but rather to clearly identify potential dangers and manage them accordingly. You'll need to understand and accurately estimate the level of risk in any particular undertaking, and weigh that danger and possible consequences against the rewards of proceeding.

The trick is not to get good at getting out of truly perilous situations, but rather to avoid them in the first place. Obviously, there is always risk in kayaking, but the goal should be to minimize it, and above all, to recognize potential risk. Constantly play the "what if" game. Imagine many different scenarios and follow them through to a logical or worst-case conclusion. Be prepared for dire outcomes and look as far ahead as you can—not just at the section immediately in front of you. The ocean is a highly changeable environment and seldom has static conditions. Recognizing the potential for danger is the first, most fundamental step in avoiding it.

There is sometimes a huge difference between perceived risk and actual risk. Paddling in big rolling swell can seem very intimidating, but if the swell is not breaking, the wind is low and there is little current action, paddling in big swell has very little inherent risk as long as you have a sheltered place to land. If, on the other hand, the beach that you intend to land on is unprotected, steep, and receiving the full power of these same big swells, then big waves will be breaking violently on shore, and this presents a very high degree of actual risk.

When assessing risk, consider as many factors as you can. Key considerations are weather, sea conditions, air and especially water temperature. Confidence, conditioning and the skill level of paddlers, preparedness of the group and proximity to good landing sites are all important issues. Consider the resources available, remoteness of the setting and finally the value of the whole enterprise. Is it worth the risk? If the answer comes back even close to "no", bag the mission and change your plans.

Risk assessment is a tricky thing. The rewards of paddling rough water are different for each person, and comfort levels can vary tremendously. It's also important to remember that confidence is far from a constant. What looks totally acceptable to me one day, may not seem like such a great idea the next. The feature or conditions haven't changed, I have. Listen to that sage little voice in your head and heed its warnings, especially when it's telling you: "don't!"

Draw on local knowledge and have a pre-paddling discussion to ensure that everyone is clear on routes and contingency plans.

Navigation

It's important to note that this book assumes that you have a significant understanding of and expertise in the use of charts, compasses and standard navigation techniques. If you are unsure or unpracticed in this area, look for Lee Moyer's excellent book: *Sea Kayaking Navigation Simplified*, or take a course through a well-established school or club.

Obviously, knowing where you are and where you are going are extremely important. But if you are planning on paddling in exposed conditions, or areas subject to strong currents, a boxed lunch and a chart will not be nearly enough. Weather patterns are very localized and each place tends to have its own patterns and pitfalls. Tides, tide currents, wind direction and velocity, swell height and direction will all play a huge role in determining what conditions you are likely to encounter. Expert knowledge is also a great help, and local fishers or boaters who know the area well can provide invaluable input.

The ocean is ever changing, so monitor conditions constantly. Keep asking yourself questions – "Is the wind picking up or dropping? How does what I see fit with the forecast? What are the currents doing? What will they be doing in an hour? What will happen to conditions when the current reverses? Where will the group be by slack tide? Is the group on schedule?" All these questions and more should be rolling around in your head as you monitor conditions and constantly re-assess your situation.

Another challenge is interpreting distances as they relate to time paddling. The chart below is a great, quick visual aid. You can even copy it and have it laminated, so it can live on your fore deck for easy reference.

Bear in mind that you'll still need to guess at the forward speed that you are making (which can be seriously hampered by wind, current, or fatigue). A group of relative beginners will cruise around 2 knots per hour in ideal conditions. A strong group will cruise closer to 3 knots. Very fit paddlers who are consciously looking to cover distance may average closer to 4 knots.

	TRAVELING SPEED (PER HOUR)				
	2 KNOTS	2.5 KNOTS	3 KNOTS	3.5 KNOTS	4 KNOTS
0.1	3 min	2.4 min	2 min	1.7 min	1.5 min
0.2	6 min	4.8 min	4 min	3.4 min	3 min
0.3	9 min	7.2 min	6 min	5.1 min	4.5 min
0.4	12 min	9.6 min	8 min	6.8 min	6 min
0.5	15 min	12 min	10 min	8.5 min	7.5 min
0.6	18 min	14.4 min	12 min	10.2 min	9 min
0.7	21 min	16.8 min	14 min	12 min	10.5 min
0.8	24 min	19.2 min	16 min	13.7 min	12 min
0.9	27 min	21.6 min	18 min	15.4 min	13.5 min
1	30 min	24 min	20 min	17 min	15 min
2	60 min	48 min	40 min	34 min	30 min
3	90 min	72 min	60 min	51 min	45 min
4	120 min	96 min	80 min	68 min	60 min
5	150 min	120 min	100 min	86 min	75 min

DISTANCE IN NAUTICAL MILES

Relating distance to time is essential to navigation. As an example: if you know that the hidden bay that you wish to camp in that evening is 1 nautical mile down the coast, and that your group will average about 3 knots, you can confidently expect to be very close to your destination after 20 minutes of paddling. This concept can elegantly be expressed in a mathematical formula. Our distance (D) traveled is equal to the speed (S) we kayak, multiplied by the time (T, expressed in hours) we spend paddling. The resulting equation is $D = ST$. Likewise, $T=D/S$ and $S=D/T$.

It is often preferable to work in units of minutes instead of units of hours, so we can modify the formula. If T = time expressed in hours, and t = time expressed in minutes, then $T = t/60$ and $60T = t$.

So it follows that $60D = St$

And $S = 60D/t$

And $t = 60D/S$

Try a few examples with the above formulas and you'll quickly see that it's easy to calculate distances and speeds relative to time in minutes.

Remember that any calculation of time and distance must be based solely on "speed made good". Speed made good refers to the distance actually paddled in prevailing conditions, and not the speed that the craft would have achieved in perfectly calm winds and flat water. In other words, because wind, waves and current all play such a major role in either slowing or speeding the progress of a kayak across the water, you must accurately reflect the true speed achieved between two points, and not how hard

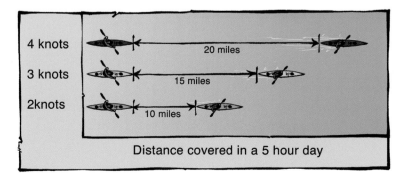

4 knots 20 miles

3 knots 15 miles

2knots 10 miles

Distance covered in a 5 hour day

Okisollo Rapids, Quadra Island area, British Columbia, Canada.

you are paddling. For more about this, see the sections on *Vectors* and *Dealing with Headwinds* in Chapter 4.

The final observation is how terribly important your watch is. A clock of some kind is a terrifically useful piece of navigational gear. Always wear a watch when you're on the water. It doesn't matter if you keep it on your wrist or stick it on your PFD, just get in the habit of recording times relative to minutes on the water. It will do wonders for your navigation skills.

Play Destinations

Finding a spot to push your limits is always exciting, but it's important to make sure that you maximize your safety-to-fun ratio by selecting appropriate play destinations. The ideal play spot is a short exciting section with plenty of safer water all around it.

A tidal rip that produces standing waves in a constricted channel is a good example. With a strong tidal exchange, big waves can form, but in the right spot, a swim will only result in being flushed into a wider, calmer body of water where a rescue is a simple process. Due to the speed of the current, it may be very hard or even impossible to get back up to the wave, but this would still represent a safe play spot. However, you do have to know and research each location—some channels generate deadly whirlpools, well know for sinking even large boats.

The right beach-break can also be a pretty benign play spot. A nice gradual sandy bottom with small to medium-sized waves and no rip tides is an awesome playground for paddlers of all levels. However, the action of strong currents on an otherwise perfect beach can make it a dangerous place. A steep beach will yield nasty dumping surf, which jacks up and crashes quickly with violent and destructive results. A rocky bottom or shoreline will make the likelihood of injury far higher. Be well aware that swell height can change quickly with an increase in wind. As always, do not assume that conditions will remain stable. Tide height also has an effect on surf. Rocks can become exposed, and the nature of the waves can change as different parts of the beach are exposed

or covered. Just because you have experienced nice, mellow surf at a location on one particular day is no guarantee that conditions are consistently friendly there.

Down-wind runs are fantastic fun, because they give you the opportunity to pick up surf rides on wind waves and link successive rides together. The distance that can be quickly covered under ideal down-wind conditions is amazing. In these contexts, you aren't looking at a small, contained area of play, but play conditions that prevail over a longer coastal section. For this reason, it is important to keep an eye on the other members of the group and stay close. It is all too easy to get caught up in the fun of surfing and lose track of one another. In most rescues, it is getting to the swimmer and not the rescue itself that takes the most time. The best down-wind runs offer a good sheltered landing destination, where coming ashore is both easy and guaranteed, even if conditions pick up over the course of the paddle.

Playing is always good fun and one of the main reasons we all paddle. What is kayaking if not play? Just be sure to choose an appropriate spot to goof off, and remember to conserve more than enough energy for the paddle home.

Bail-out Options and Contingency Plans

When planing any kayak trip, consider bail-outs on your proposed route. Simply put, these are "Plan B" options, or contingency plans.

Make note of beaches and other takeouts along your proposed route that would make good secondary targets. Be prepared to fall off your original itinerary in favour of an easier, safer one. It is the inability or unwillingness to accept conditions and adapt to them that most often gets us in trouble.

Wind is the single biggest factor when paddling, and it constantly teaches us humility. I have heard countless stories of paddlers fighting extremely high winds for many exhausting hours because they were married to a particular schedule and route. The temptation may be to expend a huge amount of energy, paddling into a headwind in scary seas, for very little distance gained—possibly leaving you too tired to enjoy the next phase or other aspects of the trip. Often, turning with the wind and working with it will get you to an alternate takeout or campsite—or you can always elect not to paddle at all.

For multi-day trips, pad your schedule with extra days, in case you encounter rough conditions or other adversity. On day trips, make sure that you have plenty of daylight hours in which to accomplish your route.

Your bail-out plan should consist of both alternate routes and timeframes. The idea is to maximize options. Most bad decisions stem from a feeling of having no other viable options, and being held to only one possible course of action.

Float Plans

Once you have established a route and schedule, draw up a float plan. This is as important to do for daytrips as it is for multi-day trips.

The float plan's job is to give potential search parties a good idea of your intended route, should you fail to arrive at your destination on time. This need not be a fancy piece of work. It only needs to communicate where you intend to travel, when you will likely be at the different waypoints along the route, and whom you will be traveling with. You can also note the number and colours of the boats on the trip. Include possible bail-out plans and approximate timeframes for travel. Be sure to communicate the changeable nature of your plans, because you definitely don't want to feel constrained to hit the schedule precisely on time, regardless of conditions. Include mobile phone numbers if available and set contact times for calls if desired. Finally, file the plan with a third party who will not be going on the trip.

A float plan is an easy way to give search-and-rescue teams a huge advantage should you go missing. By keying your route to a timeframe, you provide a clear picture of your intended movements and schedule. The result is a much more focused search pattern, which is far more likely to succeed than an attempt to search every inch of every coastline anywhere near where you might have paddled.

A float plan is also a simple courtesy, easily extended to your loved ones, who may tend to worry about you when you're away at sea.

Paddling Solo

The idea of paddling solo is often dismissed as a silly and dangerous notion. For me, paddling alone is simply a different kind of kayak trip. If I didn't paddle solo, there are quite a few wonderful journeys that I would have missed out on.

Obviously, kayaking alone does require a somewhat different mindset than paddling with even just one other person (while a group of three or four is probably safest). It is true that there is a smaller margin for error when alone, and the burden of decision-making is solely on your shoulders. Ultimately, it is probably deeply personal character traits that will determine whether you are someone who will enjoy paddling solo or not.

If you do decide to kayak alone, you should have a bombproof roll, solid paddling skills, good knowledge of the conditions you will likely encounter and the route you will travel, and a conservative attitude. When alone, it takes very little to create a dangerous situation. Without a paddling partner to lend a hand, even a minor mishap can quickly become a life-threatening scenario.

Some solo paddlers employ not only a paddle leash, but a tether that connects them to their boats as well. Such is the danger of becoming separated from one's kayak when alone in a remote location without the possibility of rescue—it should be viewed as

A float plan outlines your intended route and approximate schedule.

a potentially lethal mishap and a very real danger. Wear both the tether and the paddle leash when at sea, and then remove them when entering the surf zone to avoid possible entanglement in case you tumble or swim in crashing waves.

If you lean toward the invincible "I would absolutely never come out of my boat" school of thinking, I would suggest that you are not ready to paddle alone. If, however, you start from the realization that anything can happen, that a swim when paddling solo could be fatal, and with a determination to reduce all possible risks, then you probably are a good candidate for paddling alone.

My abiding respect for the ocean is never as clearly etched or as keenly felt as when I am traveling solo. Experiences seem a little more vivid and challenges overcome taste a little sweeter. This heightened sense of awareness is surely due to the close proximity of very real, tangible risk.

ROUGH WATER RESCUES

The primary goal in any rescue is very simple: to quickly and reliably get all involved to safety. That's it. In a rescue situation, outcome is the abiding concern, not the flawless execution of any particular rescue technique. In other words, there are no points for style! If it works, can performed quickly, safely and consistently even in rough conditions, then it's a great rescue technique.

Remember that while the rescuer obviously has a distinct role

The ultimate rescue is a dependable roll.

in any rescue scenario, you also have a role if you are the person being rescued. Rather than being a passive "victim", the person in trouble should actively participate in the rescue. First, keep your essential gear together if you can. Hang on to both your paddle and kayak. Even in light wind, waves or current, gear can float away quickly, making retrieval and rescue more difficult and time-consuming. While the rescuer is in charge of the situation, the swimmer should follow instructions and assertively engage in the rescue process; a rescue is a team effort.

The rescue techniques presented here assume the use of kayaks with fore and aft bulkheads and waterproof hatches. Bulkheads are the watertight walls that prevent the ends of a kayak from filling with water if it capsizes. If the whole volume of a composite kayak fills with water, the boat will sink and head straight to the bottom. If only one end fills, the kayak will go vertical. Both these scenarios make rescue far more difficult. Air bags can also be used in the ends of boats to displace water, but they must be very securely anchored in the kayak so that they can't come out even when subjected to the effects of waves and current. If your kayak does not have plenty of flotation in both the bow and stern, get one that does!

Rescues That Keep Paddlers in Their Boats

Any capsize recovery technique that keeps a paddler in his or her boat is vastly superior to one that involves a swim, no matter how brief. In rough conditions, becoming separated from your boat is a very distinct possibility, and losing your kayak is a very scary proposition. The best way to stay in contact with your boat is to keep your butt glued to the seat.

The only effective way of keeping your butt in your boat is to learn to roll reliably. So to put it bluntly, if you plan to paddle hard stuff, you owe it to yourself (and those you paddle with) to learn to roll.

AIDED RE-ENTRY RESCUES

Aided rescues in rough seas can be terrifically hard on gear, and potentially hazardous to fingers, hands and feet. In fact, just about any body part can all too easily get pinched between boats. In pitching seas, rafting up with another kayak is going to be a bouncy experience. Boats will rise and fall with waves and smash together alarmingly. Perform re-entries quickly to minimize immersion time and to re-establish a safe distance between boaters as soon as possible.

Most of the time, once you are swimming in the water, your number one priority is to keep your paddle and kayak together. Your second priority is to get back in your boat. Keeping a good grip on both your kayak and paddle will allow the quickest rescue. If a paddle drifts only a short distance away, it may be lost for good. If for some reason you must choose between your boat and your paddle, keep a death grip on your boat. After all, you have a spare paddle on your stern, don't you?

It is a sobering thought, but it must be understood and acknowledged that in some conditions, no aided-rescue has much chance of success. Seas can become so rough that performing a rescue (other than a roll) is impossible. Every paddler is ostensibly on their own and alone in these extreme conditions. You may be able to see a partner nearby, but it does not mean that they can lend meaningful assistance. This of course means that you must paddle within your means, and respect the awesome power of the sea in all its changeable moods.

Bow Tip-Out or T-Rescue

The bow tip-out rescue is an all-around strong rescue technique. It is quick, dependable and can be performed reliably in most heavy conditions. It also has the great advantage of emptying

The bow tip-out is a strong an all-around strong rescue technique.

the capsized kayak of water before the swimmer re-enters it. The bow tip-out should be one of the cornerstones of any kayaker's primary rescue techniques.

To perform a bow tip-out, the rescuer approaches the bow of the capsized kayak. Ideally, the rescuer will position themselves perpendicular to the capsized boat, creating a T formation. Bear in mind however, that rescues in heavy seas do not tend to be ideal. So forget the perfect T, and just get to the capsized boat's bow. Get a good grip on the bow. Don't be afraid to commit your weight onto the capsized boat. If possible, get a grip on the bow's grab handle. Direct the swimmer to the stern of their kayak, where they can press down on the stern keel of the kayak. This will raise the bow of the kayak and break the seal created by the cockpit against the water. Once the bow "pops" free of the surface of the water, decisively yank the bow forward across your spray deck and front deck. The capsized kayak remains upside down this whole time, so when the boat is placed on an angle, the water inside will flow down toward the stern bulkhead, and drain from the boat. The rescuer then spins the kayak upright, taking care that if there's a rudder, it doesn't contact the swimmer's face. The rescuer can now pull the swimmer's kayak in parallel to their own boat and brace it so the swimmer can re-enter the boat. As

always, commit fully to bracing the swimmer's kayak by leaning your body weight onto their boat to stabilize it.

One of the challenges in any aided rescue is managing paddles. I generally keep mine in my lap, where I can pin it between the front edge of my PFD, the spray deck and my elbows. The swimmer's paddle must be secured as well and can be stuffed under a deck shock cord. Paddle leashes are wonderful things when doing a rescue—you can drop your paddle at anytime with no fear of it floating away.

If conditions are tough and a bow tip-out is looking like an epic undertaking, simply get alongside the capsized boat, grab it and flip it upright. Now stabilize it by leaning your weight aggressively onto the empty kayak. The swimmer can then re-enter the boat and pump the water out.

Flipping the capsized boat upright quickly will tend to scoop less water into the cockpit, but in tough conditions, water will get in anyway as waves slosh over the sides. Don't worry about clearing water until the swimmer is firmly back in their kayak, with spray deck in place.

As always, there are no points for style—so stay focused on the outcome. The goal is to get a swimmer out of the cold water and back in their kayak as quickly as possible.

To stabilize a kayak for re-entry, securely grip the perimeter lines and commit fully to leaning onto the empty boat.

To re-enter a kayak from the water use a powerful kick and push up with your arms to haul your chest up onto the stern deck.

Re-Entries

In an aided rescue, there are a number of ways for a swimmer to get back into their righted kayak. While some of these strategies for re-entry are easier to perform than others, there is no doubt that an agile, fit swimmer will have a much higher success ratio than an exhausted, out-of-shape swimmer. All of the techniques involve the rescuer positioning their kayak parallel to the swimmer's boat. The rescuer then stabilizes the other boat by committing their weight onto it and establishing a firm grip of the coaming or deck lines with both hands.

Assisted Side-by-Side Re-Entry

One of the quickest ways to get back into your boat is with the side-by-side re-entry. In this case, as the swimmer, you will approach the kayak from the outside, just behind the cockpit. Grab the cockpit rim, and with a powerful kick of the legs, pull up with the arms and heave your chest right up on top of your kayak's stern deck. Get a hand over onto the rescuer's boat to spread the load and help keep the kayaks together. Facing the stern, you can then lift your legs into the cockpit and slide into the cockpit while twisting your body back into a sitting position. Stay low throughout the maneuver in order to maximize stability.

As a rescuer, be sure not to release your grip until the swimmer is ready, with their spray deck on and paddle at the ready.

Sling Re-Entry

The assisted side-by-side re-entry described above can be supplemented with the use of a sling.

Slings are nothing more than tubular webbing or floating rope tied in a loop, but they can be helpful for getting back into a boat. The loop can be secured around your cockpit coaming, or tied onto deck hardware or interior components of the cockpit. The idea is to create a step up into the boat. The sling is a great tool for paddlers who need that helping hand to get back into their boat.

If this is a system that you intend to use in challenging conditions, then you need to practice it often so it's fast to deploy and reliable. A rescue system that requires any fiddling around with knots or complicated setups will not work in rough seas.

Staying low, face the stern of your boat and
slide your legs into the cockpit.

Twist into a sitting position and get your
spray deck back on.

Face Up Re-Entry

The face up re-entry doesn't require quite as much explosive power as the side-by-side re-entry, but places the swimmer between the two kayaks, which is potentially dangerous in rough seas. For this reason, I prefer the side-by-side re-entry.

For a face up re-entry, as the swimmer you'll start at the stern end of your kayak, in between your boat and the rescuer's boats positioned parallel to each other. Throw an arm over the end of each kayak and then hook one leg up and into the cockpit of your boat. Swing your second leg up and into the cockpit and then wiggle your way into the seat.

Scoop

If none of the above re-entries are working for some reason, then the scoop might be the only option. The concept behind the scoop is that the swimmer floats back into the kayak, and then relies on the rescuer to rotate them upright.

This rescue is exceedingly difficult in rough conditions, but it may prove to be the only option with swimmers who are totally exhausted, injured or otherwise incapable of re-entering their boats from the water. Even an injured paddler can be floated into their boat, the cockpit pumped out and the kayak stabilized while it is towed to safety. If you can get an injured or compromised paddler out of the cold water, they will be in a far better position

The face up re-entry requires less explosive power from the swimmer.

The scoop re-entry requires the least exertion from the swimmer.

to weather the challenge of a tow to shore.

As the rescuer, you'll set yourself up as usual, although you won't want to empty out the kayak first in this case. In fact, you'll want to flood it. With the kayak on its side, the swimmer re-enters the boat by floating in feet first, while pulling themselves in by the cockpit coaming. The swimmer needs to get themselves as far into the kayak as possible, ideally beyond their foot pedals, and then they will lean all the way back onto their stern deck to lower their center of gravity as much as possible. The rescuer then pulls up hard on the coaming to right the swamped kayak. Continuing to stabilize their boat, the swimmer can sit back up, get their spray deck in place and start pumping the water out.

Removing Water from the Boat

After re-entering a swamped kayak, you'll need to pump the water out of your boat. The most popular pumps are hand-held designs because they're affordable and because they can be easily shared. With your spray deck fitted on the kayak, the pump slides inside the tunnel of your spray deck, or through an upturned corner. The downside of these pumps is that it takes both hands to operate them, which is tricky when conditions are rough. With a partner to stabilize the kayak, hand pumps work passably well. When alone, they are very difficult or impossible to use in rough conditions.

You can also get deck mounted or foot pumps, which are built-

Emptying a swamped kayak with a hand pump is time-consuming and hard work.

in to your kayak. The nice thing about these systems is that you can keep your spray deck fully sealed and they typically only take a single hand or foot to operate. The downside is that they aren't as easily shared, although if fitted with a suitably long intake tube,

---

NOTE

The only way to successfully stabilize a paddling partner's boat is to truly commit to it! Lean right over and drape yourself over their deck. Try to get the peak of their deck in your armpit. Grab hold of their coaming, or better still, grip the perimeter deck lines. By grabbing the deck lines, you are far less likely to get kicked or kneed in the hands as the swimmer re-enters their kayak. Either way, establish a serious grip and lean onto the boat to stabilize it. No half measures will do—commit!

---

they can be used to pump out someone else's kayak.

No matter what bailing system you use, it takes a LONG time and a lot of energy to pump out a flooded cockpit, and when the conditions are rough, it will take even longer. Depending on the situation, it might be necessary for the rescuer to continue lending their support until all the pumping is done.

Tows

Towing another boat isn't always part of a rescue scenario. Sometimes you may decide to put a kayak under tow simply to lend a helping hand to a tired paddler in strong current or wind. Towing is also a great way to assist an injured or seasick paddler.

In rough water applications, towlines are most often used for short distance tows aimed at getting a swimmer out of immediate danger. The most common scenario is retrieving a paddler who has capsized and is swimming in close proximity to a rocky or otherwise unfriendly shoreline. Because waves will be actively breaking up against cliffs or the shore, but not further out toward sea, you can swoop in, attach a line to a kayak and/or grab the paddler and then tow it/them back out to deeper water.

Whatever the situation, as the rescuer you have a lot of towing options to choose from and a wide variety of towline systems available to you.

All towlines should have a carabiner on one end for clipping onto another kayak. A quick release buckle that lets you unhook the whole system is also essential because it allows you to break free of the rig with a simple flick of your wrist in case you get tangled. The best tow setups are integrated into a PFD. With this approach, the tow system is always on your body, and not an extra bit of gear that you can forget or decide not to bring. Another important advantage of the PFD tow design is the fact that the quick release buckle is solidly fixed in one place where it is always within easy reach. Waist-worn tow belts can easily rotate on the torso, making it difficult to locate the quick release buckle in an emergency.

The leash portion of the tow system can be short or long. Short leashes, around 3-10 feet (1-3 meters) in length are called cow tails. They're great tools because they are so quick and easy to deploy, without the inherent risk of entanglement that is presented with long lines. Cow tails usually consist of tubular webbing with a length of shock cord sewn inside. The webbing is immensely strong and the shock cord causes the webbing to bunch up, shortening the cow tail's overall length when not under load. A carabiner is attached to one end, while the other is anchored to the quick release strap on your rescue-specific PFD. Generally, cow tails are only effective for very short distance tows.

Long leashes are around 30-45 feet (9-14 meters) in length, and are far better for towing over longer distances and in rough conditions. For distance tows, it is important to have enough space between the lead boat and the boat being towed because boat collisions are a real risk, particularly in following seas when the towed boat can otherwise easily surf down a wave and into the lead kayak. Long leashes are a little more unwieldy, particularly trying to stuff them away after use. Sometimes rather than re-stuffing a long line back into its bag, it is easier to stuff the line between your chest and PFD, at least until you get to some calmer water.

Towing is very taxing and the decision to tow another kayak a long distance should not be undertaken lightly. In rough conditions or when fighting current or wind, it is exhausting. Usually, short distance tows are all that are required, whether it's to extract a paddler from immediate danger or to reunite them with their boat. Also be aware that deploying long tow lines in breaking surf or powerful rapids is very dangerous and should be avoided due to the risk of entanglement.

Towing from Danger (Extraction)

As we know, even a big rolling swell isn't likely to hurt us when we're surrounded by deep open water. But when that swell hits the shoreline—watch out! Even when small waves break, they can represent a hazard to paddlers who are hugging the shoreline,

The classic in-line tow formation.

A contact tow is fast to setup because it doesn't require any specialized gear.

exploring rock gardens or sea caves. Rebounding waves coming off cliffs or wave sets colliding with rocks and reefs can cause very confused wave patterns, and it is not uncommon for a paddler to be knocked over in these conditions.

When a paddler capsizes and ends up in close proximity to a sheer cliff or shoreline that is completely unsuitable for landing, a quick tow to deeper water is the best rescue. This is known as a "tow from danger" or an "extraction". In these conditions it is typically extremely difficult or even impossible for a swimmer to swim their own boat out to deeper water, because the waves will be strongly pushing debris (like expensive kayaks and their owners) towards shore and the sharp rocks.

As rescuer, you will sprint in, timing it as best you can to avoid the worst of the wave action, clip a tow line into the capsized kayak, and tow it and the swimmer out to deeper water. This is a maneuver that needs to be performed as quickly as possible. Clip into either the bow or stern, it doesn't matter which. The

swimmer, as half of the rescue effort, is often in the best position to actually clip the carabiner to the capsized kayak. Flipping the capsized boat upright will make it far easier to tow, but do not waste time on this if it is proving too difficult. Hanging around in the impact zone while trying to get things perfectly organized is a recipe for disaster. Get in fast, and get out faster!

Spend as little time maneuvering your boat around as possible. It is often easiest to sprint in to the capsized kayak, clip in, and then reverse powerfully out, away from the shoreline. By eliminating the need to turn your kayak around, you save valuable time and get the swimmer and kayak into deeper water faster. This is another good reason to develop a strong and confident back stroke.

If there are several strong paddlers in your group, have one rescuer grab the capsized kayak and another pick up the swimmer. Once relieved of their capsized kayak, a swimmer is often capable of clearing the shoreline on their own power too.

This is a tricky rescue. You need to clearly assess whether

you will fare any better up against the rocks than the capsized paddler did. Do not charge in blindly if there is little likelihood of success—two swimmers are not better than one. Timing and speed of execution are the key ingredients. If you feel that you can only grab either the swimmer or the boat, and both are in immediate and serious danger, go for the swimmer. Using a longer towline, you may be able to stay further off the shore, and throw the line to the swimmer, towing them out that way.

Contact Tow

A contact tow is a really fast way to move another paddler who is still in their kayak. This technique is best for short distances, and it's great for quickly getting another kayaker away from rocks or any other hazard. It's fast to set up because it doesn't rely on a towline or any other specific hardware.

If you're the rescuer, pull up to the other boat, facing the opposite direction. The paddler to be towed then gets a hold of the rescuer's fore deck, committing to this grip, and drapes themselves over the rescuer's boat. The rescuer then paddles the makeshift raft forward. As the rescuer, you might want to cheat your grip to one side so that you can reach over the other boat more easily to get your stroke in.

NOTE

The contact tow can be augmented by the rescuer using a cow tail attached to the bow of the kayak under tow. This makes it easier to hold the raft formation together while towing.

The beauty of this tow is the sheer speed of deployment. You can start towing the second that you get into position, without fumbling with equipment. Obviously, you're not going to want to tow someone like this very far, but it's a great way to get a paddling partner out of immediate danger quickly.

In-Line Tow

The in-line tow is the most basic towing formation. As the rescuer, simply clip your boat to the bow of the boat to be towed. You'll want to use a towline with some stretch, because this will make for a smoother tow with fewer jolts and jarring. The towed boat should be far enough behind the lead kayak that its bow won't contact the lead boat. For additional speed and power, a second

With an assisted in-line tow, several paddlers share the strain of pulling another kayak.

The rafted tow is ideal for assisting a seriously motion sick or otherwise incapacitated paddler who is in danger of capsizing.

The piggy-back tow gets a swimmer's core out of the water, reducing the dangerous effects of full cold water immersion.

NOTE

The contact tow and in-line tow can be combined to do what is called a "rafted in-line" tow, which is perfect if the paddler being towed needs constant attention, such as in the case of serious injury or seasickness. The tow boat must pull two kayaks: the invalid's, and a support paddler's. Thread your towline through the bow loop of the invalid's boat, and then clip onto the bow or stern loop of the support kayak for an in-line rafted tow. The raft setup allows the support paddler to provide boat stability and encouragement to the invalid, and to assist with communication while both are under tow.

tow boat can be added to the front of the formation to create a mini conga-line for additional speed and power. This also serves to spread the considerable strain of towing to two paddlers.

Piggy-Back

If you find yourself having to tow a swimmer, the best way to do it is to have them climb up onto the stern of your boat and grab your waist or the cockpit coaming. The swimmer lies face down,

NOTE

You can also tow a swimmer on the bow of your boat instead of your stern. The swimmer remains in the water and hugs your bow, wrapping their arms and legs around your boat, with their back to the oncoming water. This method is only good for short distances. Use it when you need to save the time it would take to get the swimmer onto your stern – sometimes a quick and simple maneuver like this is all you need to reunite a swimmer with their kayak.

with their chest hard against the deck, and a leg trailing in the water on either side of the boat. The swimmer should keep their center of gravity as low as possible so that the kayak will retain maximum stability while carrying the extra passenger. This technique works well because it keeps the swimmer mostly out of the water, which reduces drag and also keeps the swimmer the warmest.

Swimming with a Paddle

Swimming effectively while maintaining a firm grip on your paddle may seem like a pretty tall order, but the paddle can in fact be a big asset.

If you find yourself swimming, you must get actively involved in your own rescue. This may mean covering some distance in the water, and it may even mean towing your boat at the end of your towline—but it will always mean firmly holding on to your paddle. The way to generate some power in this ungainly situation is to use your paddle exactly as you would if you were sitting in your kayak. Use either a back stroke or forward stroke. In-water strokes when you are swimming generate a surprising amount of power and turn your paddle from an encumbrance to an asset. Practice these in-water paddle strokes to find out what works best for you, and even practice towing your boat this way. You'll be amazed at how effectively you can do it.

SOLO RE-ENTRIES & SELF-RESCUES

Before getting into specific self-rescue techniques, it's important to understand that whatever caused you to swim in the first place

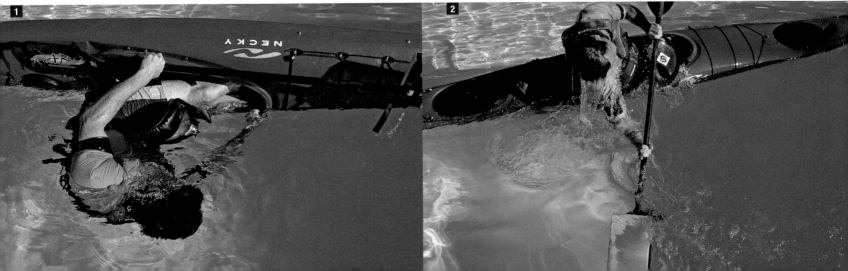

Re-enter your overturned kayak while holding your paddle along side the cockpit.

Once securely back in the kayak, roll the boat upright – a paddle float can be used for extra flotation.

will probably make a self-rescue difficult, if not impossible. I repeat: if you plan to paddle hard stuff, you owe it to yourself (and those you paddle with) to learn to roll. Still, the more self-rescue techniques you arm yourself with, the better chance you have of dealing effectively with any situations that arise.

Re-Entry and Roll

If for some reason you miss your roll and end up swimming (it happens to all of us sooner or later), you can re-enter your kayak while it's upside down, and then roll back up.

The key to performing a successful re-enter and roll is establishing adequate contact in the cockpit of your capsized kayak.

If you want to roll up on your right, position yourself by the cockpit, on the right side of the capsized boat (this is actually port side of the overturned kayak). Place your paddle along the edge of the cockpit (port side), so that you can grip your paddle and the coaming with your left hand. Your right hand reaches across to the far side of the coaming.

Take a deep breath, and swing your feet up into the cockpit. It's like doing a somersault. I will usually feed my legs part way in, take one last breath, and then go for the full re-entry.

This is the crux of the maneuver: be sure to pull your butt completely into the seat, and then get your knees, and at least one foot, firmly braced in place. Then roll. If you fail to get a good grip on the boat with your lower body, you'll be unable to roll successfully.

Once you've rolled the boat upright, you'll need to pump the water out, or you may opt to make a dash for shore if you're close enough and empty the water there.

If you missed your roll in the first place, it probably means that your roll isn't as strong as it could be. To beef up your re-enter and roll, you can supplement the roll portion by affixing a paddle float to your paddle. By attaching a paddle float to your rolling blade, you'll get much more support for your roll. You'll also have a solid brace to use while pumping the water out of your kayak.

The key to the deceptively simple scramble re-entry is to stay low and practice often.

A paddle float rescue offers little chance of success in rough conditions.

The only disadvantage is that deploying the float will mean a little more time in the water.

Scramble

The scramble is exactly what it sounds like. It refers to climbing up on top of your kayak, and then slipping into the cockpit. In rough water, you'll need to do it as quickly as possible because your kayak will be very unstable until you get your butt back down into the boat.

After flipping your kayak upright, approach your boat from the side at the stern. Place your paddle across the stern deck, perpendicular to your boat. Facing the bow, hold the paddle and the back of the cockpit rim with one hand and reach across to the other side of the boat with your free hand. Now pull yourself up onto the boat and, staying as low as possible, throw a leg over the kayak so that you're straddling it. You can now use your paddle to scull for support as you slide forward to the seat and drop your butt into the cockpit. Once your butt is in the seat you will be quite stable. Pull your feet in, get the deck on, pump water out, and head for home.

Some paddlers become amazingly good at this rescue. With practice, and depending on what boat you paddle, it can become a very fast, and amazingly dependable maneuver for mild conditions. While it's probably not going to succeed in rough seas, it does work in surf, as long as you are getting enough time between sets to set up and then scramble.

The scramble is simple and represents a really fast self-rescue that requires no extra or specialized gear. While it is far from the ultimate rough water rescue, it is well worth the time to develop and practice this technique.

Paddle Float

The paddle float rescue is mentioned here only because it is the most widely promoted solo self-rescue in North America. I have included it in a book on rough water paddling only to stress the fact that it is an unacceptably weak self-rescue technique in rough conditions and stands little chance of success in violent seas. For these reasons, it is completely inappropriate for rough water paddling. If it is your primary solo self-rescue, you should never consider paddling alone in anything but calm waters.

Post-Rescue Considerations

A swim can be an emotionally and physically exhausting experience, especially if the conditions are rough and the water is cold, so don't assume that you can plug a swimmer back into their kayak and forge ahead as if nothing happened.

If a member of your group feels that they are paddling close to the limit of their abilities, they may be highly stressed and tire quickly. Fatigue and exposure are very real dangers. Do not underestimate the potential negative effects of capsizing, even if a quick and efficient rescue has been performed. Even very mild hypothermia can dramatically compromise a kayaker's endurance and abilities. In its early stages, the debilitating effects of hypothermia can also be very hard to recognize.

Sometimes the best course of action may be to head to shore for a rest. As already noted, it's a great idea to always carry the basic gear that will allow you to spend an unplanned night out in case you get caught by bad weather or experience other unexpected difficulties. A rest break is also a great time to put some of this gear to use. A tarp to break the wind, a steaming hot drink and changing out of wet clothes and into dry warm ones can all be greatly reassuring and energizing for everyone. Just make sure that folks aren't getting colder by standing around on a windswept beach.

Also keep in mind that paddlers will sometimes ignore what their bodies are telling them because they don't want to appear weak to the other paddlers in their group. The adrenaline that results from a dramatic capsize in big seas can also mask injuries, so always carefully observe behavior as well as noting verbal responses. Hypothermia, fatigue and stress can all cloud judgment and result in poor decision-making. So, if you have any doubt about someone's condition, including your own, ask for a break or cut the trip short. Similarly, when others on the trip ask for a rest or a change in plans because they are running out of steam, respect the request and adapt to the needs of the group.

4

MOVING WATER

CURRENTS & TIDES SURFING
ROCK GARDENS / CAVES / SURGE CHANNELS PADDLING IN THE WIND

Water is an incredibly dynamic medium, and it is always in motion. Its movements may be small and difficult to discern, or monumental and ferociously destructive. Even a seemingly immobile glacier, made of frozen water, is constantly on the move. How water moves (hydrodynamics) is an amazingly complex science, but for our purposes we will limit ourselves to considering the fundamental effects of tides, currents, geography and wind on water conditions.

CURRENTS & TIDES

Currents and tides exert profound and complex influence on the movement of water. If you want to seek out more challenging paddling, you need to be ready to deal with the effects of tides and currents. Most importantly, you'll also need to be able to anticipate and predict these changes with a reasonable degree of accuracy.

In the simplest terms, tides are the movement of water up and down on a vertical plane; currents are the movement of water back and forth on a horizontal plane. Tides and ocean currents are caused by the gravitational effects of the moon, sun and planets on water. The moon has the greatest effect, the sun has the second greatest effect, and the planets have a small effect. Because all bodies of water are subject to the gravitational pull of the moon, they all have tides, but on smaller bodies of water like lakes, the effect is so small that it is unnoticeable. The larger the body of water, the more pronounced the effect.

While tides and tidal currents are implicitly linked, the two are not one and the same. The timing and height of tides has little or no useful correlation to the direction and speed of tidal currents. For the purposes of understanding how these affect kayak navigation, we will consider tides and ocean currents as separate concerns.

Happily, both tides and tidal currents can be predicted with good accuracy using a tide and current atlas, and appropriate marine charts. Keep in mind that these are updated regularly, and are different for each calendar year—so don't get caught trying to use outdated tide or current tables.

When the water is rising it's called a flood tide, and when it's dropping, it's an ebb tide. Not surprisingly, what's called high tide is the point where the water is at its highest, and low tide is the point when the water is at its lowest. There are roughly 6.5 hours between these two times. There are two sets of tides per day: a "major tide", which has a greater disparity between the high and low tides, and a "minor tide", which has a lesser disparity between high and low tides. This pattern repeats itself approximately every 24 hours. The whole tidal pattern itself changes with the phases of the moon, synchronized with the 28-day lunar cycle. Because tides can vary greatly, they have a big impact on the accessibility of certain areas. It is not uncommon for channels that have plenty of water at high tide to become completely dry at low tide. Marine charts provide this information, and will let you plan accordingly.

The "Reversing Falls" of St John, New Brunswick, Canada, are caused by the enormous tides in the Bay of Fundy – the biggest tides in the world.

Tidal currents have the greatest impact on a sea kayaker, however. Tidal currents are caused by the massive amount of water (associated with the changing tide) being forced around islands and up channels. When this water gets pushed through constricted channels, you'll often get strong currents, and in some cases, large rapids with towering waves and whirlpools. For any tidal flow, there is a time of maximum flood, when water is flooding in at its greatest speed, and a time of maximum ebb, when water is flowing back out at its highest speed. "Slack tide" refers to the time when the water is between the flood and ebb, and at its calmest. A paddler can choose to travel at slack for the easiest conditions, or use the flow of water for play or a helping push in one direction.

To paddle effectively and comfortably in strong currents, there are a few absolutely key skills that you need to develop. Strong currents can either be really intimidating or—if you master these skills, exercise sound judgment, and research when and when not to navigate tidal passages—they can be a lot of fun.

Planning Trips Around Tides and Currents

No paddling trip is ever totally predictable. Water is far too dynamic and exciting a medium for that. There will always be many factors that will affect your time on the water and in camp, but some of these factors can be carefully analyzed and accurately predicted long before you set off, like tides and tidal currents.

When planning a kayak trip, lay out your route and timeframe, and then carefully consider the effects of tides and currents along that route using up-to-date tide and current tables. In some areas, there may be little to consider; tidal currents may be very weak or virtually nonexistent, or the difference in tide heights may be small and inconsequential. In other areas, you will be able to anticipate with some certainty that you'll encounter challenging tidal rips and violent whitewater.

Tide information is important primarily for establishing water depth. Some inter-tidal areas like marshes, mud flats, bays and channels will run dry at low tides and prevent passage. In areas with big tides, or on very gradual beaches, landing at high tide will leave you stranded a long way from water should you want to head out again after the water recedes. Conversely, landing on the same long gradual beaches at low tide will require a long portage to get boats safely above the coming high tide line.

TIP

One current that does have a direct and obvious link to tide heights is generated at river mouths, where fresh water pours into the sea. When tides are at their lowest, the difference in elevation between the river mouth and the surface of the sea is at its greatest. This increased gradient will generate more current at the river mouth. If you are considering paddling a coastal route, where you will encounter a swift running river (swollen by heavy rain for instance) flowing into the sea, and your schedule will have you arriving at the river mouth at low tide, expect strong currents! Depending on the volume and speed of the river, these currents can be forceful and sweep far out to sea.

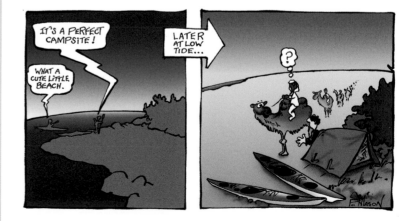

Depending on geography, the time of day, and the speed of currents, channels can present mellow riffles appropriate for play, or scary rapids with towering waves and deep whirlpools.

It is also very helpful to simply know if the next high tide will be higher or lower than the last one. When landing at a beach for the night, it is generally easy to see the last high tide line. A clear line along the sand, and debris deposited on the beach, will outline the furthest advance of the water at the apex of the last high tide. If you know, by looking it up in your tide book, that the next high tide is lower than the last, you can confidently use the existing high tide line as a guide. Pitch your tent above the last high tide line and you should be fine. However, if the next high tide is going to be higher than the last, head for higher ground!

Be aware that things like storms and swell generated by wind can cause water to travel much further up a beach (especially shores with a long gradual slope) than it would in calm conditions. So use tide height as a rough guide only—the wake from just one passing super tanker can ruin an otherwise great night's sleep.

Tidal currents represent a far greater risk to paddlers than tides ever do. Marine charts, guidebooks and local knowledge will help you identify rip tides and tidal passages. A current book or atlas will let you ascertain the timing, speed and direction of the tidal exchange in particular spots. It's important to understand that

although you may have slack tide in one location, it is possible that only a few miles away, the current may still be moving. The movement of currents is not only complex, it is often really counter-intuitive too, so it's best to consult a current atlas and avoid guesswork—with currents, your guesses will very often be completely wrong.

To help you estimate current speeds in a tidal passage, the "Rule of Thirds" is a very useful technique. The Rule of Thirds breaks the flood or ebb tide currents into three segments of approximately one hour, and assigns a current speed to each of these hours.

As we know, the ebb or flood tidal currents last about 6.5 hours. Currents go from slack (zero movement, or a current under 0.5 knots), to maximum speed, building over approximately 3 hours. The current then begins to slow again, and as it decreases in speed, heading toward the next slack, this deceleration also takes about 3 hours. The Rule of Thirds states that relative to the total maximum current speed, the current jumps 50% the first hour, 90% the second hour, 100% the third hour. The current then decelerates to slack in the same order.

So, if we have a tidal passage that will flood (for instance) at a maximum of 10 knots, we can assume the following pattern of speed:

Hour 0   0% slack current, turning to flood
         approximately 0 knots

Hour 1   50% increasing current speed (flooding)
         approximately 5 knots

Hour 2   90% increasing current speed (flooding)
         approximately 9 knots

Hour 3   100% or maximum current speed (flooding)
         approximately 10 knots

Hour 4   90% decreasing current speed (flooding)
         approximately 9 knots

Hour 5   50% decreasing current speed (flooding)
         approximately 5 knots

Hour 6   0% slack current, turning to ebb
         approximately 0 knots

The same formula holds true for ebb tide currents.

It can also be quite helpful to get a rough estimate of how long a slack current is likely to last. The "Slow Water Rule" is useful for this purpose. By establishing the maximum flood and maximum ebb (expressed in knots) for either side of the turn that we are interested in, we can calculate the approximate duration of slack water (current under 0.5 knots).

In a current atlas, look up the maximum flows before and after the slack in question.

Say that the turn in question is at 0840, with a maximum flood of +4 at 0540, and a maximum ebb after it being -3 at 1200.

60 / 4 = 15 minutes

60 / 3 = 20 minutes

15 + 20 = 35 minutes

So the period of slack water where currents will be less than 0.5 knots during the turn will be about 35 minutes.

When ebb and flood currents are moving faster, the duration of slack will be shorter. Let's say that in the same scenario

Even moderate tidal currents can greatly change the nature of a section of water and seriously affect your progress through the area.

mentioned above, flows were +10 and −12 knots respectively on the flood and ebb.

60 / 10 = 6 minutes

60 / 12 = 5 minutes

6 + 5 = 11 minutes

In this instance, the period of slack water during the turn from flood to ebb current will only be approximately 11 minutes.

Current information is invaluable when planning a trip through a tidal passage. Armed with this knowledge, you can paddle through safely at slack, or better still, use the current for a helping push by paddling through just before or just after slack. Even potentially deadly tidal passages that have overturned large vessels can be safely navigated by kayak, as long as it is attempted at the correct time. Plan to get to questionable spots early, before slack tide. This strategy is best because it will give you a chance to watch the current and confirm your calculations and timing. Let the current slow to a speed that you are comfortable with, and then head in. For example, if you head in just before slack, you know that from that point forward, the current speed will only decrease until it switches direction and then accelerates the other way.

Finally, be aware that current speed is far from the sole indicator of a tidal passage or rip current's potential for danger. Bottom geography, local winds and shorelines all contribute significantly. As always, do your homework and study guidebooks as well as seeking out local knowledge.

When dealing with currents that don't represent a hazard to navigation, you'll of course want to time things so that you're paddling with the current in order to make the most progress. For example, if you're doing a round trip on a day paddle, time things so that you paddle away with the current, then turn and make your way back home when the tide changes so that you're still paddling with the current.

Marine charts provide very useful visual information about the direction of tidal currents. The arrows on a chart indicate the direction of flow. The arrows with "feathers" indicate the direction of flooding water, and a nice mnemonic device to help you remember is "F for feather, F for flood". The arrows without feathers show the direction of ebbing tidal currents.

Remember that not all regions on the planet neatly conform to a predictable pattern of tides, so, whether you are looking to play in moving water or avoid it altogether, it's necessary to consult a recent tide and current book to accurately predict times and heights of tides and currents.

To peel into or out of an eddy, start with a good head of steam and a 45-degree angle relative to the eddy line.

As you cross the eddy line, tilt your boat into your turn. Stay balanced over your kayak while using a low brace to control the turn.

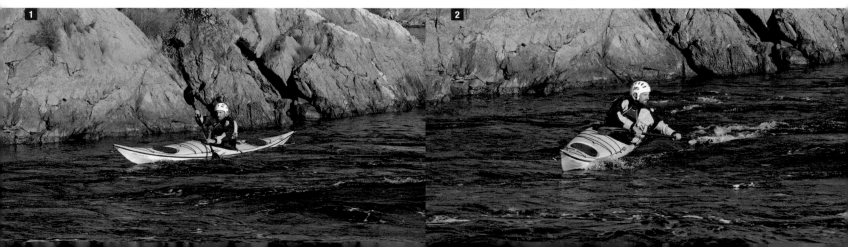

NOTE

Big storms can disrupt the flows of tidal currents and reduce the accuracy of current table predictions. The final word is always going to rest with a visual appraisal of the area once you are on the scene. If it looks bad, but all the math seems to work, trust your senses and make decisions accordingly.

Basic Current Dynamics

To safely navigate current, it's necessary to understand the basic components and behavior of moving water.

Both tidal and river rapids can be broken into two parts. There's the main current, and there are eddies. Eddies are relatively calm areas of water that form behind the features that obstruct the main current, such as rocks. As the main current is deflected around the obstruction, an eddy is formed as water curls around and circles back in behind it. For this reason, eddies have their own current, which moves in the opposite direction to the main current.

Where the eddy current and the main current meet, you get an eddy line. Eddy lines are without a doubt the most unstable and unpredictable places to be. They're usually fairly easily identified and are often accompanied by whirlpools and other swirling water. The stronger the eddy and main currents are, the stronger and choppier the eddy line will be.

As a general rule, your goal when paddling through current is to spend the least amount of time on eddy lines. Sometimes you can just point your boat downstream or upstream and paddle, staying in the main current and avoiding eddy lines all together. Keeping your boat straight and your body forward, you can paddle through some pretty big waves this way. Other times though, it will be desirable to work your way in and out of eddies and use the current to help you get to where you want to go.

Crossing Eddy Lines

To paddle competently in current, you will definitely need to become confident crossing eddy lines. Crossing an eddy line into or out of an eddy is called an eddy turn. If you can do a solid low or high brace lean turn on flat water, then you've already got the individual skills that you'll need to do an eddy turn. It's simply a matter of combining timing, edging and your lean turn, together with the right plan of action.

Maintain the downstream tilt on your boat until the turn is finished.

Sit up straight or lean slightly forward throughout the eddy turn.

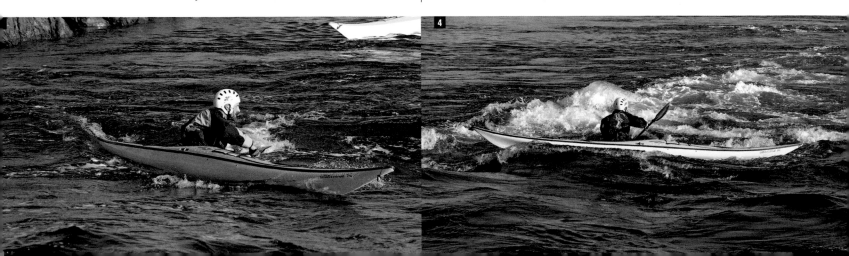

To ferry across current, start with forward speed
and a strong upstream angle.

The stronger the current is, the more directly
upstream you'll need to be pointed.

The first thing to know is that when crossing into the main current from an eddy, you always want to cross the eddy line with your boat on about a 45-degree angle pointing upstream or up current. It is very important that you carry some forward speed into this maneuver, because you want to cut across the eddy line decisively and not end up stranded in the confused water between the two currents.

As soon as your bow crosses the eddy line, the main current will grab it and pull it downstream or with the current. If you're not prepared for this, it can flip your boat very quickly. The way to prepare for this is to tilt your boat downstream—edge it on the downstream side—as you cross the eddy line, in the direction of your turn, just as you'd edge your skis to carve a turn, or how you'd lean a motorcycle into a corner.

As you cross the eddy line with some decisive speed and edge your boat downstream, keep your paddle at the ready in the low brace or high brace position on the downstream side of your kayak. Recognize the low brace lean turn that you practiced on flat water? Using this technique you should be able to perform a smooth turn either into an eddy or into the main current so that you can continue downstream. When you are heading downstream and crossing the eddy line from the main current

to the eddy current, the only difference is that your stern will of course be pointing upstream; but you will still cross the eddy line with decisive speed, on about a 45-degree angle, and edge your boat on the downstream side.

The timing of the transition from edge to edge is critical for smooth entries and exits from current, and with a little practice it will become second nature. Note that in very strong currents, boat tilt will have to be increased in order to free the upstream edge and prevent it from loading and flipping your kayak. It's not a bad idea to exaggerate the tilt, especially when practicing, in order to get really comfortable with your boat on edge. More tilt will also give you a tighter turn.

Ferrying

The ability to use current to help you get where you need to go will transform your ability to maneuver in moving water. Instead of blindly fighting the current, for example, use a ferry angle.

Ferrying is a technique used to cross current laterally, and is accomplished by paddling with your kayak angled upstream so that during your crossing, you make enough upstream progress to counteract the speed at which the current sweeps you downstream.

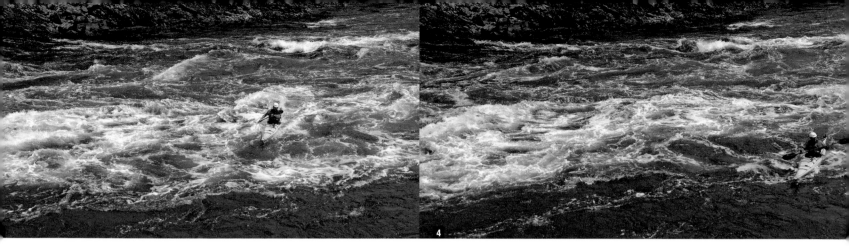

As you get closer to your destination, relax your upstream angle so that you can build lateral momentum across the current and into the eddy.

Don't relax until you're safely in the eddy. Remember that the eddy line is the most unstable location.

In milder current, you can point yourself more directly across to your destination, but when the current gets stronger, you'll have to keep a fairly aggressive upstream angle on your kayak to fight the current that will otherwise pull you downstream. You'll also need to keep your boat tilted on a slight downstream angle throughout your ferry. This is to ensure that water doesn't pile up on the upstream edge of your kayak and flip your boat.

If you're starting your ferry from an eddy, you'll want to cross the eddy line like you did for an eddy turn, but with a bit more upstream angle so that your bow doesn't get pulled downstream. (There is a brief point as you cross when half your boat will be in the eddy current and half of it will be in the main current—and if you don't have a good upstream angle, enough speed, and are not edging, you'll spin or flip.) As you cross the eddy line, you may need a few sweep strokes on the downstream side of your boat to keep your bow pointed upstream.

Using the eddy turn and ferry techniques, you should be able to navigate through surprisingly strong current without too much trouble. Of course, rescue situations are complicated with the addition of current, so make sure that you're not getting in over your head.

Next, we're going to look at how to stay on track when ferrying across expansive sections of water with current.

Ranges

When crossing current over a long distance, it can be pretty difficult to stay on a straight-line course from point of departure to destination. But this straight A to B course is the most efficient. As we all know, the shortest distance between two points is a straight line.

A range or transit (these two terms mean the same thing) gives a paddler reliable on-the-fly visual feedback about course headings relative to lateral drift. It might sound complicated, but it's really easy and very useful on longer crossings, and handy for short ones too. Taking a range provides a paddler with a safeguard that can easily prevent drifting off course due to current or wind.

To establish a range, pick two stationary reference points that are off in the distance and roughly on your course heading. Your two points need to be some distance apart, with one closer and one further away from your position, but roughly in line with your direction of travel. By watching how these two reference points move relative to one another, you can instantly gauge if you are drifting off course.

Say you pick a mountain peak in the far distance, and a dead tree on the shoreline as your reference points. If the mountain is moving left relative to the tree, then you are drifting off course to

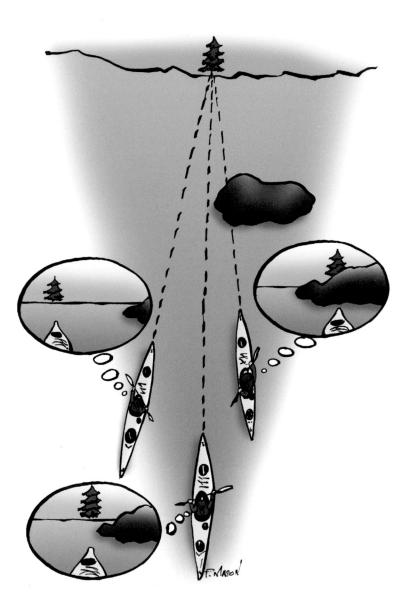

A range provides great visual feedback about course heading relative to lateral drift.

the left. If the mountain is moving right relative to the tree, then you are drifting right. If the two reference points stay aligned, then you are on course and traveling in a straight line.

Ranges are great for staying on course on long crossings. Taking a range allows a paddler to set and maintain the appropriate ferry angle, and it will keep you heading to your chosen destination in a straight line even if the effects of current and winds are changing constantly.

Lines of Position

Lines of position can help you figure out your location. This is a handy skill that should become an almost unconscious part of your navigation.

Take a range from clearly identifiable landmarks that you can see on your marine chart. This will create a line of position for each range, from one landmark to the next. If you can establish two or more lines of position from your location, the point where the lines intersect with your course will show your position on the chart. Of course, this can also be done using a single known landmark as a reference point and a compass bearing, a technique known as triangulation. Whichever way you do it, the more lines of position that you establish or the more bearings you can take, the higher the degree of accuracy in determining your position.

This concept can also be used to gauge your progress over a crossing. By mapping out a range and its line of position, you can see where it will intersect your course. Your chart gives you precise information for distances, so ranges can give you a good sense of how far you've traveled and how far you have yet to go.

It's a great idea to get into the habit of taking ranges and establishing lines of position. With a little attention on these techniques, you'll feel far more confident finding your way through unfamiliar landscapes.

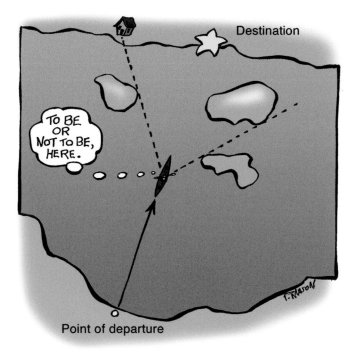

Destination

TO BE OR NOT TO BE, HERE.

Point of departure

"When I hit the point in my crossing where I can establish both my 'lines of position', then I'll know that I'm about half way."

Vectors

If you find yourself lacking landmarks, as in heavy fog for instance, taking a range will be impossible. Vectors are another way of establishing a good idea of the amount of ferry angle that you will require for crossing a channel in current, and they're a great tool for working out how long a crossing will likely take.

Rather than depending on a line of sight, vectors require some chart work. Draw your course on your chart. Next, establish the direction and speed of current that you will encounter during your crossing. Using calipers, a ruler or a scrap of paper, create units of measurement that correspond to one nautical mile on your chart. From your point of departure, draw a vector that is

parallel to the direction of current (in this example, slightly north of due west), and equal to its speed (3 knots).

Now here's the rub: for this technique to work, you need to know how fast you paddle. For this exercise, we are going to use a group that paddles at a quick 4 knots (any speed can be used, as long as it is constant—just adjust your calipers accordingly). From the end of your "current speed" vector, connect the "paddling speed" vector to your original course line. The resulting angle will give you the appropriate ferry angle for the crossing. By transposing the "paddling speed" vector angle through the center of your chart's compass rose, you will be able to read the correct heading to compensate for the action of the 3 knots of current. The point where the "paddling speed" vector intersects your course will give you the distance traveled in one hour and your "speed made good".

"Speed made good" refers to the distance actually paddled in prevailing conditions, not the speed that the craft would have traveled at in calm water. In this example, our paddling speed is

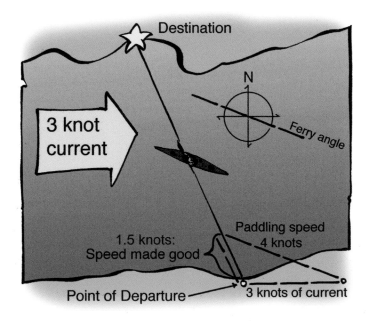

Destination

N

3 knot current

Ferry angle

1.5 knots: Speed made good

Paddling speed 4 knots

Point of Departure

3 knots of current

Surfing a big green standing wave is one of the sweetest feelings to be had in a kayak.

4 knots, but due to the effect of current, our speed made good is only around 1.5 knots.

In the above scenario, battling a 3 knot current is going to reduce our paddling speed of 4 knots to a "speed made good" of a mere 1.5 knots. This means that a crossing that is only a little further than 6 nautical miles will take over 4 hours to complete. In my opinion, this is a great example of a crossing that would benefit from some more planning. Paddling at slack or even when the current reverses would make a huge difference to the time required to complete the crossing, and the energy expended in its undertaking.

If you do decide to make a trip of the sort illustrated above, you will be much better served to cross on a course that is more perpendicular to the current. Although this course won't land you at your final destination, it will significantly cut down the time that you spend in the channel, because less of your paddling energy

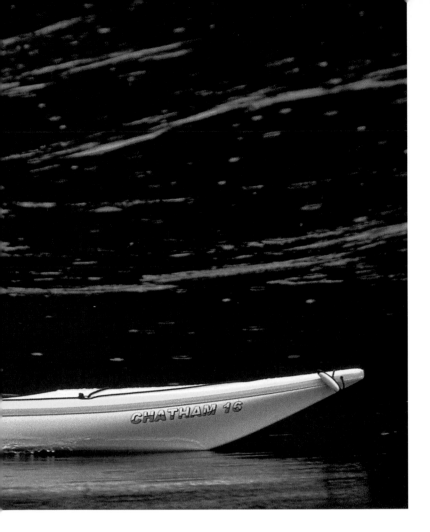

The lesson to take away from this is that while the shortest distance between two points is a straight line, that straight line may not represent the fastest and best path to the goal.

A final, interesting note about vectors is the fact that the units of measurement don't actually need to relate to the scale of your chart. If a random unit of measurement is used consistently throughout the process, the resulting angles and relations created will still yield the same results. Just be sure to remember that you are using a completely different scale to your charts, so don't confuse the two. If this last statement makes no sense, try it and see what you get. If it's still confusing, just revert to always using your chart's scale as the basis for all your measurements.

Surfing Standing Waves

When swift moving water flows over the geography on the sea floor (or riverbed), standing waves, holes and rapids are sometimes formed. The size, nature and power of these resulting features will vary greatly with changes in water depth, speed and volume of the passing water, and the shape of the underlying bottom geography that is generating the disturbance in the first place. While it is often prudent to maneuver around these features, it can also be a lot of fun to play in them. Standing waves, in particular, can offer up some great rides.

Because the water is rushing past quickly, but the bottom geography creating the disturbance is stationary, we end up with an unmoving or "standing" wave. This doesn't mean that they aren't dynamic. Standing waves often change from green to breaking, and will sometimes even disappear altogether, only to reform again moments later.

Because these features are a result of current, waves will not build quickly and then crash the way ocean swell will as it explodes on shore. Instead, standing waves will gradually build and shrink over hours, just as the tidal currents do.

To surf a standing wave you'll first need to use your ability to

will be spent fighting the current. Once on the opposite side, you can hug the shore for the rest of the way to your destination. The action of the current will be far weaker along the shoreline, and there may even be back eddies that will make paddling against the current far easier. Either way, you can expect the overall paddling time to be less by electing to avoid a direct route, and you'll also spend considerably less time in the open channel where you are at more risk.

It's extremely important to know what's lurking behind and downstream from any feature you plan to surf. In large tidal rapids, boils and whirlpools are quite common.

ferry in current, in order to maneuver yourself into position. You might have to catch the wave on-the-fly, sprinting on to it from upstream, as you are carried down by the current. Or there may be a convenient eddy beside the wave, which will let you ferry out directly onto the face. Selecting the right wave and getting to the sweet spot on it is sometimes the trickiest part. Refer to the *Surfing* section of this chapter for more information about the mechanics of catching and surfing a wave.

When picking a wave to surf, be sure to take note of what's found downstream. The bigger, better waves are often above nasty rapids that can take all the fun out of an otherwise sweet surf session. Have an exit strategy ready for getting off the wave, and be sure to consider the consequences of a swim. Also remember that features will build and ebb with the tidal currents, so be very aware of what currents are doing and when they will be at their most powerful.

Rescues in Current

If you are going to paddle in strong currents, then obviously you must also be prepared to perform rescues in them. Whether you are performing the rescue, or are the one having to be fished out, you need to have a clear plan of action for when things start to go wrong.

Performing rescues in current can, of course, be very challenging and each situation will require a unique solution. One of the biggest factors that will dictate your action plan is the number of rescuers available. If there is only a single rescuer on hand, one of the biggest concerns will usually be keeping the loose gear and the swimmer close together. When a swimmer has a "garage sale" and spews all their gear across the surface of fast moving water, it can be a little daunting.

Rapids generated by tidal current are usually fairly short in length, so often the best thing for the swimmer to do is to hang onto their paddle and kayak and weather the worst of the rapid in the water. As the rescuer, you can provide a lot of added security to the swimmer by offering an end of your kayak for them to hold on to as they float through the rapid. If the rapid isn't long and it's easy to predict where the empty kayak will end up, or if the rapid is particularly violent and the capsized kayak presents a major hazard as it gets tossed around by waves, the best option may be for the swimmer to let go of their kayak and hold on to the rescuer's boat. The pieces can be reunited and a rescue can be performed once things start to calm down.

A system of two rescuers works best in current. One rescuer can attend to the swimmer, while the other gathers loose gear. When you all reach calmer water, the gear and swimmer can be brought back together.

In rough water, gathering the pieces can take some time, but once rafted up, a re-entry should be very quick. While performing the rescue, it's very easy to suffer "tunnel vision" and focus too intently on the sole task of getting a paddler back in their boat—which is important of course, but it's also important to keep an eye on surroundings in the process. When rafted-up, our ability to maneuver is about zero so it's key to pay attention to where we are being taken by the current. It's amazing how far and fast you can be swept downstream. Keep your eyes open for rocks, shoals, reefs, and other marine traffic. Other vessels, from high-powered jet boats to lumbering tug boats pulling barges, represent a very serious hazard and can come up on you very quickly.

If you're close to shore, and a clearly defined and relatively calm eddy is available, it's a great idea to perform the re-entry there. A swimmer should swim aggressively for any good eddy or they can be towed into one along with their kayak. This will get you out

Wherever large volumes of water are in motion, powerful hydraulics are likely to form.

of the main flow of the current and stop you from all going any farther downstream. You now have lots of time to perform the rescue and take a break from the mayhem of the rapids.

Kayaking in strong current can be a real blast. Waves build, eddy lines form, holes appear, and the swiftly moving water creates a truly dynamic paddling environment. But this playground can definitely turn mean. It's important to approach tidal rapids with a conservative attitude. Take your time and carefully scout the conditions. Be willing to say no if you aren't confident in your ability to navigate through the rapid safely.

SURFING

Entering the surf zone is one of the most exciting and physically demanding activities that a sea kayaker can undertake. Surf is also one of the absolute best places to build "real world" rough water paddling skills. So get out there!

Of course, when you're playing with crashing waves and shallow water or rocky coastlines, it also has the potential to be dangerous, so make sure that you pick an appropriate place to play. The best introduction to kayak surfing may well be to take a course through an established club or paddling school. In challenging surf, paddle with other experienced kayakers who are comfortable in the conditions and who are able to assist in case you swim. Commit to a team approach where all paddlers keep an eye on one another. You should be confident of your ability to self-rescue (meaning, have a bombproof roll), and always be prepared to rescue someone else.

Unlike whitewater boats or surf-specific designs, sea kayaks are designed more for efficiency in covering long distances, rather than the ultimate carving performance on a steep wave. But it's just this efficiency that allows a sea kayak to pick up many rides that a whitewater boat never could. Sea kayaks can catch smaller waves earlier and much further off the beach.

Ocean swell is another great place to look for a ride. Even far

from the beach, swell can roll across the sea, offering up sweet rides to whoever can catch them. There is nothing quite like linking up several consecutive rides on wind waves.

Learning to surf waves, be they standing waves created by current, wind swell, or beach break, is a key skill. Control in surf will allow you to safely navigate otherwise intimidating conditions—and the ability to use the power of the water to help you get where you're going, instead of fighting it, will make you a far more efficient and graceful paddler.

The Formation of Waves and "Sticky-Out Bits"

Surf waves are formed when ocean swells created by offshore storms hit shallower sections of water. Wave size is generally measured by the size of their face, from crest to trough. The overall size of waves is one thing to consider, but the nature of the break is also important. A long evenly sloping beach with little angle will generate surf that builds gradually. Wave faces will tend

Gradually sloping beaches generate more benign surf conditions, while steep beaches create vicious dumping surf.

to get predictably steeper and break, spilling from the crest of the wave. Even fairly large waves are relatively forgiving on this type of beach.

By contrast, a steep beach will generate surf that "jacks up" and "dumps" very quickly. The sudden collapse of the wave focuses all its power in one crash, so waves breaking on steep beaches pack a real punch and are unforgiving in the extreme. The sheer angle of these beaches also makes landing very difficult. Add dumping surf as an ingredient and you've got a recipe for serious punishment. Sometimes it's best to continue down the coast to a more sheltered spot, where waves are smaller and more benign.

In deep water, even large swells will not break unless strong wind is acting on the sea. So although these moving mountains of water can seem very threatening, it isn't until nearing shore or shallow water that they will get steeper and break.

Basically, waves want to be parallel to the shoreline when they meet it, so incoming swell will actually wrap around obstacles. You'll see this in the way that the power from ocean swells concentrates and is most intense at points and headlands. To simplify: beware of geographical "sticky-out bits"! Conversely, this same effect means that the power of waves is dissipated in formations like bays, creating calmer water conditions.

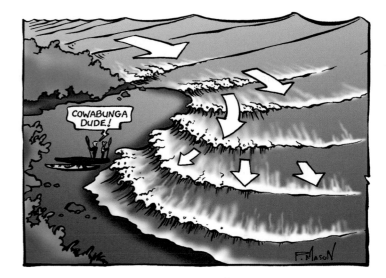

Beware of headlands or "sticky-out bits" where the intensity and power of waves and wind are magnified.

Swells and waves will break in shallow waters, like those created by reefs or submerged rocks.

Waves will also rebound off of cliff faces or breakwaters. These reflected or rebounding waves combine with the incoming swell, increasing overall wave size and power close to the reflecting surface, and creating very rough and confused sea conditions. In some cases, a reflected wave will meet an incoming wave, and as both break, the energy of their collision will send water exploding into the air. These are called clapotis waves and while they are very spectacular, they are also a sobering sight to any kayaker considering paddling near them. Because clapotis are generated by two colliding waves, the timing of the impact must be perfect in order to create the effect. This means that it may be an infrequently and irregularly occurring event. In some ways this makes clapotis more dangerous, because they can be so unpredictable. Although it may initially seem counter-intuitive, heading further out to sea rather than hugging the shoreline is usually the best course to take around reefs, cliffs, points and headlands, to avoid the confused and unpredictable water that these formations often have in proximity to them.

The rugged west coast of Nootka Island, British Columbia, Canada.

The sea kayaking community is a small one, and through personal accounts and articles, it is often possible to review the circumstances surrounding accidents that have befallen paddlers. It is incredible how often things go wrong at points or headlands. These areas are potentially very dangerous because both the effects of swell and waves, as well as wind, are greatly intensified in locations where land juts out into the water. So remember to beware, and always respect the "sticky-out bits".

Rip Tides and Rip Currents

Although the pounding of breaking waves on a beach represents a clear hazard in and of itself, rip tides are a far less visually obvious danger. Rip currents form when water that has been pushed up on a beach by breaking waves is pulled back out by gravity. Because waves may continually push more water up the slope of the beach, there can be a lot of water searching for the quickest way out. Since rip tides can be tricky to spot and are surprisingly powerful, they are the primary cause of swimmer rescues at surf beaches.

If you're in control, you can use rip currents to help get past the shore break. If you're playing in the waves and catching rides in, a rip tide can be like an escalator that gives you a free ride back out, so you can do it all over again. But if you're overwhelmed by their power, or find yourself swimming, rip currents can be very dangerous.

To escape from a rip current, you need to swim, or paddle perpendicular to the current until you're free from it. This generally means heading in a direction parallel to the shoreline. If you try to simply head straight in, you can find yourself ineffectually fighting a powerful current the whole way, and possibly dangerously exhausting yourself.

Many rip currents are well known by the local paddlers or surfers, so it's worth asking around. As always, guidebooks as well as expert local knowledge are huge assets when heading to a new destination.

Rip currents can be difficult to spot, but create powerful flows that can quickly push the unwary into deeper water.

lull between waves. This is easiest when you have the assistance of a paddling partner who can stand in the shallows and hold your boat perpendicular to the incoming waves. Without this person, it's easy for your kayak to get turned sideways as you get in. When dealing with bigger surf, it's usually easiest to get into your boat just at the edge of the incoming water. This will give you as much time as you need to get settled in your boat. You'll then need to push yourself out until you're in water that is deep enough to paddle away. Of course, a fellow paddler can also give you a push or pull that will be especially useful if you're paddling a loaded boat. As you push yourself, or get pushed into the water, your main goal is to control your bow angle so that your kayak stays perpendicular to the waves. It is also very important to be aware of any lateral movement that you may be making relative to the launch site. If one wave washes under you and picks you up, but you don't make it off the beach, you'll usually still be moved sideways. Depending on currents and the beach, sometimes you can be swept quite far sideways by a single wave. This is important to note, because on small beaches, you may have only one attempt to get clear before the current sweeps you into rocks.

Launching in Surf

Launching in surf can be pretty tricky and very intimidating, although it's actually easier than it might initially seem. In fact, it comes as a surprise to many to hear that it's easier to paddle out through moderate surf than it is to come back through it to land on the beach. The key is keeping your boat perpendicular to the waves and paddling hard directly at them. With an aggressive approach like this, you'll be amazed at the waves that you can punch through.

Your first challenge will be getting into your boat. Waves come in sets, so take your time to watch and analyze the rhythm of the incoming waves so that you can time your departure with a lull in wave activity. Depending on the conditions, you may be able to float your boat in about a foot of water and hop into it during the

Take the time to carefully study your environment before launching.

Breaking through Surf

As with launching in surf, the key to paddling out through surf is timing your break-out for a sprint during the lull between wave sets. Keep studying the waves as they roll in until you've established a pattern. Be sure to look for weak spots in the incoming waves too, because there is sometimes a preferred path out through the breakers.

Once you go for it, commit yourself to the job. Keep your boat perpendicular to the waves and drive yourself aggressively forward.

Commit to breaking through surf—lean forward and plant a powerful forward stroke just as you hit the wave.

TIP

If you are totally confident of making it overtop of a steep wave, you can choose to turn your kayak slightly off of its perpendicular course to the incoming surf. Passing over a steep wave on an angle will greatly reduce the violence of your kayak's landing after it launches off the top of the wave and slams into the water on the backside. The downside of using this technique is that if you don't make it over the wave before it starts breaking, the angle on your kayak will likely cause your boat to be pulled right down into the trough. Once in the trough and off-angle, it will be much more difficult to maintain control and to reset the angle. Trial and error in the form of practice is the only way to figure out the right combination of angle and force required for different sizes and types of waves.

If you haven't done this before, you will probably surprise yourself with the size of wave you can comfortably break through. When busting through a wave that is breaking, or that is about to break, the most important thing to do is to lean forward and plant a powerful forward stroke just as you hit the wave. This stroke will pull you through and at the same time act like a brace. In bigger surf, it's a good idea to tuck your head behind your arm as the wave breaks over you. This will soften the impact of the water against your face and head. Make sure your paddle stays planted deeply in the water so that you can pull yourself right through and over the backside of the wave.

As a final note, make absolutely sure that you're well past the breaking point of the waves. It's easy to think that you're in the clear, when really a set has just passed. Making this mistake will mean that you'll find yourself with your guard down right in the impact zone of the biggest waves.

Surfing, or Playing in Surf

Aside from being one of the coolest feelings in the world, surfing is an important skill to learn for a number of other reasons. Being able to control your surf will let you make controlled landings when the conditions aren't perfectly flat. It also lets you ride wind waves, which can increase your paddling speed dramatically and allow you to cover distances faster.

Because sea kayaks are so efficient at moving forward, you can start your ride on pretty gentle swells, before they become steeper and the waves start breaking. To catch a wave, line up perpendicular to its face, and as it approaches, paddle aggressively forward. After about three to five strokes you should reach your maximum speed, at which time the wave should have reached

you and started to pick up your stern. This will actually mean waiting until the wave is quite close before paddling forward. As you feel your stern being picked up by the wave, lean forward and continue with a few more powerful strokes, until you're sure that you've caught the wave. Once you're surfing, you can stop stroking, because gravity will keep you on the face of the wave. You'll then want to shift your weight back a bit, to help lighten your bow, and use a stern rudder to control your direction.

As mentioned in the section on the *Stern Rudder* in Chapter 2, the stern pry is considerably more powerful than the stern draw. For this reason, you'll alternate between stern pries to keep your boat on track. Remember to plant your paddle deeply with your upper body aggressively rotated, which will allow you to use the power of your upper torso and protect your shoulders by keeping your hands in front of your body in the power position.

As the wave continues to get steeper and then breaks, chances are that your sea kayak will start turning out of your control. The bow will likely dive, or purl underwater, and dynamically deflect to the left or right. When this happens, don't bother trying to

A controlled side-surf is achieved with a low brace and your boat tilted into the wave. It also keeps your shoulders safe from injury.

fight it. As your bow deflects either right or left, edge your boat in that direction by shifting your weight onto the inside butt cheek and lifting the outer knee. If the wave is still green, you can carve right off of it. If it's breaking, you'll probably end up side-surfing. Side-surfing means sitting at the bottom of a breaking wave, with your boat parallel to the wave. Your weight needs to be balanced on the butt cheek on the wave side of your kayak, and your paddle should be held in a low brace or a high brace on the side of the foam pile, with your arms kept in close. If you want to move forward or backward while in a side-surf, you can do so, but you can only take strokes in the foam pile of the wave.

Side-surfing can actually be a dependable and controlled way to land, although it's important to note that once you're sideways to a breaking wave, you'll usually be locked that way until the wave completely dissipates. This is really important to understand, because it will play a large role in dictating which are good surf areas and which are dangerous ones. What happens if you get side-surfed right into shore? Is there a nice beach to re-establish control on, or is the run-out a nasty shoreline, like a rock cliff, that you could get swept right into?

Landing in Surf

Landing in surf is much more difficult than paddling out through it. In fact, surf landings consistently represent the most demanding, taxing and scary aspect of sea kayaking.

Assessing the size and nature of surf from beyond the break is also extremely difficult. So when encountering an unfamiliar surf break while touring, it pays to be very cautious. Take the time to watch and learn the rhythm and pattern of the waves as they roll in. Consider the timing of the sets, and map out the areas where waves are least powerful. Carefully scope out landing areas and consider what the run-out of an uncontrolled ride will be. As you formulate your plan, stay alert for particularly big wave sets that might roll in behind you and that could sweep you in to shore before you're ready.

Once you've made the decision to go, you really have two options. You can ride a wave right into shore, but your best option is usually to "chase" a wave in to shore. This means following on the heels of the last wave of a set. To chase a wave in, you'll let the last wave of a set pass and then sprint in behind it all the way into shore. If timed correctly, this approach negates the need to control a dynamic surf ride, or at least it will allow you to avoid the worst of the impact zone.

Once you get to shore, jump out of your boat, grab the bow, and hit the ground running. Drag your kayak well up the beach, away from the power of the waves. If you can get out of your boat and up the beach before the next wave rolls in, you will greatly reduce the potential for carnage while you exit the kayak, so proceed with a sense of urgency.

If you've got a loaded boat, you'll need to be extra cautious when landing. It will be harder to keep your boat straight while surfing in, and when you hop out, that heavy boat can really hurt someone—including you, if you end up swimming with it—if it's not controlled. Within a group planning to land through surf, the best thing to do is to have the two strongest paddlers be the first and last to go in. The rest of the group should land one at a time, and wait for the go-ahead from the person on shore. This exercise should be conducted like an air-traffic controller's dream, and not like a free-for-all. In order for this to work, everyone in your group needs to know and agree on hand and paddle signals.

If you're on shore helping people land, make sure you give incoming kayaks a wide berth. Never stand directly in front of one, try to catch one, or position yourself between a kayak and the shore. Even a small wave can pick a boat up and launch it with surprising force at your kneecaps or shins, potentially causing serious injury.

Rolling in Surf

A reliable roll is a great thing to have when dealing with surf and could be considered a necessity if you want to start actively

Ruth times the break and heads to shore.

The raw power of water in motion is irrefutable.

power will do all the rest.

In the biggest waves, you're simply going to "eat it". Stay as relaxed as possible, keep a firm grip on your boat and paddle, and get a good full breath before you get slammed. Your only option is to wait for the wave to pass over top of you, or until the trashing has mellowed out enough so that you can orient yourself and find purchase with your paddle to roll up in the foam pile.

No matter how good you get at rolling in a pool, there is no substitute for "real world" experience, so you'll want to get out there, play around and test your combat roll. Just make sure you take small and reasonable steps in doing so. Although there will undoubtedly be some humbling times, the payoffs are considerable if you're interested in doing more adventuresome sea kayaking. A reliable rough-water roll will change how you paddle, boost your confidence and open up a whole new world of paddling possibilities.

playing in the surf zone.

The first thing to know is that if you can roll in flat water, you can roll in the surf. The biggest challenge is dealing with the disorientation that often accompanies flipping in rough water, because your paddle and body will get tugged in all directions. The key is to stay as relaxed as possible while at the same time keeping a strong grip on your paddle and gripping your boat securely with your legs in their thigh hooks. In medium-sized surf, it usually won't take long before the wave passes over you, and the water calms down. You can then roll up in the calm, flat water between waves. In bigger surf, you'll probably need to roll in the wave. Believe it or not, rolling in a wave can often be easier than rolling in calm water, because the moving water can help to pull you up. The key is rolling up on the foam pile side of your kayak. In fact, rolls aided by the foam pile are not really "full" rolls. It's usually more a question of finding some support with your paddle and then hip-snapping yourself upright. The wave's

Swimmer Rescues in Surf

If someone does end up swimming in the surf zone, it will be a very challenging rescue situation. Depending on where the capsize occurs and what the nature and size of the surf is, it may be better to either tow the swimmer out of the break zone to deeper, calmer water, or bring them into shore. Depending on conditions, a rescuer may be able to dash in, clip into the boat and tow the kayak and swimmer out beyond the break, where they can perform an assisted re-entry. It can also be highly advantageous to have one rescuer tow the swimmer, while another tows the boat. This approach greatly reduces the drag that each rescue paddler has to overcome in getting out of the break zone.

If there's a long enough lull between waves or sets, it's possible to perform a fast rescue on the spot. A super-quick bow tip-out is best. Don't worry about getting every last drop out of the boat. This rescue must be performed very quickly, and the key is to get the swimmer back in their kayak as soon as possible. Even if the boat is still flooded, a paddler can often then make it to shore, or out beyond the breakers, where the boat can be fully pumped out.

Sometimes the best course of action is for the swimmer to "surf" their capsized boat in, which means hanging on to an end and swimming the kayak to shore. The waves will usually give a good boost in, although you'll need to be careful of your boat when you get close to shore.

In really big, violent surf, the best course of action is to swim aggressively away from the capsized boat. You really don't want to be tumbling out of control in a massive wave with several hundred rampaging pounds of sea kayak. A collision with a pitch-poling kayak can result in very serious injury, so forget about the boat, and get well clear of it. Concentrate on getting yourself safely to shore, and hope the boat does the same. Although you may find yourself stranded if your kayak gets destroyed on the way in, at least you will be in one piece. Remember, gear can be easily replaced, people can not!

Surf Etiquette

If you're going to go play in the surf, you need to learn to play nicely with others. Wherever there's good surf, you're likely to find board surfers and other paddlers. Follow some surfing "road rules" to avoid collisions on the water, which can be devastating due to the power and speed involved.

The single most important rule in the surf has to do with the surfing "right of way". The surfer who catches an unbroken wave first, and is closest to the breaking curl while still remaining on the green face, has the right of way. All of this is largely decided moments before anyone is actually on the wave, due to the huge importance of positioning for takeoff. A surfer is considered to have caught the wave once they have stopped paddling, kicking or stroking, and are moving down the face of the wave due to the force of gravity alone. Remember that this rule only applies to unbroken waves. A surfer has no right of way on broken waves. Catching a wave that a surfer is already on is known as "dropping in" on someone and is a cardinal sin. If you find yourself on a

wave and a surfer is on the inside of you (closer to the break than you are), get off the wave at once. Apologize at the first opportunity and try to foster communication out on the water as to who is going to take off on which wave.

While in theory it's a surfer's responsibility to avoid all swimmers, surfers or paddlers that they encounter while riding in on a wave, those paddling out through the surf must also do their very best not to interfere with incoming surfers. This might mean taking the long route out, or it could mean paddling directly into the broken sections. Never paddle straight out through "the lane" where surfers are riding waves in—you will only put everyone at risk of a collision.

Something else to consider is the advantage that kayakers have over other surfers. We can catch waves earlier than board surfers and it's easier for us to paddle back out after each surf. Show respect, wait your turn, and let the other surfers all grab a few waves.

On a final note, popular surfing areas have territorial issues that surprise many sea kayakers. Local surfers often believe that they have more right to "their waves" than others. Though this might not make a lot of sense, it's not something that you should fight. Be an ambassador for your sport and consider yourself a "guest"

This surfer has right of way.

at their surf spots. Show local paddlers and surfers respect and give them a wide berth. A friendly greeting and an "after you" mentality will go a long way to making your time in the surf more enjoyable, even if you do end up getting a few less surfs than you'd like.

ROCK GARDENS / CAVES / SURGE CHANNELS

Exploring rock gardens and sea caves, paddling through sea arches or surge channels are all activities that will demand that you blend many of the skills that we have already covered in this book. Navigating confined spaces in turbulent water requires confident, efficient strokes and precise timing. To precisely control your kayak and make it through a surge channel with a wave, make sure that you time your charge to coincide with the rush of a wave. Mistimed launches will leave you high and dry on exposed rock, scraping gelcoat off your hull, but the reward of blasting through a tight channel with perfect timing is a sweet feeling of exhilaration.

Paddling rock gardens, sea caves and surge channels will put you in very close proximity to exposed rock. Combine that with waves and rushing water and you have an excellent recipe for potentially dangerous collisions. If you choose to challenge yourself in these locations, expect to at least scrape your boat up, and you may potentially collide very heavily with rocks, so a good helmet is an essential piece of safety gear. Plastic kayaks are great in this environment because they take impacts incredibly well and endure abuse admirably. Composite kayaks, while being much tougher than most people think, are more likely to sustain heavy damage than a polymer model in the event of a serious crash.

When exploring tight, rocky channels or caves with swell or waves in the vicinity, I will often back myself in. Although this means that I need to continually look over my shoulder to check

Take-outs and launch sites are not always ideal and sometimes a seal launch is the best plan of action.

where I'm going, by facing straight out to sea, I'm in a great position to hightail it out of there if I see a big wave rolling in.

Should a heavy impact with rock be imminent, let the boat take the hit instead of your body. Even if you destroy the boat, you can always get another one. The same can't be said for an arm or head. If you are being swept into rocks while side-surfing a wave, lean aggressively into the foam pile and present your hull to the rock. Let the bottom of the kayak take the impact and shield your body from the razor-sharp, barnacle-covered rocks.

The bottom line is that paddling around rock gardens, sea caves or surge channels is a commitment and requires advanced paddling skills. You should only do so with a team of competent paddlers and you should never paddle anywhere that you wouldn't be prepared to swim out of.

Seal Launch

Shorelines without a smooth launching beach can present the biggest challenge to getting started. This is where the "seal launch" comes in, although it should be noted right off the bat that this is an advanced technique for entering the water that carries some risk with it. Stone beaches are ideal seal launch zones because you can just get in your boat, get your spray deck on, and then slide into the water using your kayak like a toboggan. Of course, this is one of those times that you'll be happy to have a plastic kayak.

Seal launching also works well for departing from steep banks like rock ledges or docks. For a successful seal launch, one of the key ingredients is commitment. A half-hearted attempt will not be as successful as one driven by a bold "bring it on" mentality.

Be sure to check the landing spot for hazards and ensure that the water is more than deep enough before you launch.

Set up with your boat at the edge of the drop with the bow hanging out over space. Be sure to get in with the centre of gravity of the boat well back so that you don't risk pitching forward unexpectedly into the water. Once you're ready, the easiest way to

ensure a good launch is to enlist the aid of a partner who can pick up the stern of your boat and give you a shove.

On big seal launches, when you actually find yourself falling towards the water instead of sliding into the water, you need to be careful with your paddle. You need to avoid landing on a big brace, which could injure your shoulder, and be careful that you don't "eat" your paddle shaft by getting it too close to your face. To avoid doing either, the best position to hold your paddle is off to the side, in a low brace position. If everything goes to plan, you will land at an angle between 45 and 65 degrees. The bow will pierce the water and then the buoyancy in the kayak will quickly drive the bow back to the surface.

If your whole group is entering the water this way, it means that the last paddler will have to launch alone, without the aid of someone else's help. This is much more difficult than an assisted launch because it is very hard to get the good push-off and speed needed to clear the stern of a long boat. It certainly works, but sometimes simply throwing the kayak over the edge and jumping in after it is easiest. A quick re-enter and roll or bow tip-out rescue at the bottom and you'll be ready to go.

The author opts for the shortest path between two points.

photo: Josh McCulloch

PADDLING IN WIND

When sea kayakers talk about "conditions", they usually have wind in mind because no other element affects us more. Wind shapes the surface of the water and dictates our progress across it. Wind is by far the single biggest factor in determining where, when, or even if, we can travel on the water.

Sir Francis Beaufort of England developed the Beaufort Wind Scale in 1805. This table gives a good, quick and concise idea of what to expect at different wind speeds.

Fetch is defined as "the unobstructed region of the ocean over which the wind blows to generate waves". In other words, fetch refers to the distance of water that prevailing winds can act upon. The greater the fetch, the larger the wind's effect. Imagine a small pond 10 feet (about 3 m) across. No matter how windy it gets, the water will remain relatively calm. Now imagine a long channel 10 feet wide by 100 miles (about 160 km) long. If the wind blows in a direction perpendicular to the channel, across its 10 feet width, little will happen. But should a strong wind be blowing straight down the direction that the channel travels, waves will form. This is a result of the increased fetch or straight-line length of the body of water. Any obstacles (like islands, peninsulas, or breakwaters) in the way of the wind will reduce fetch and the resultant action

Paddling into a strong headwind is both physically draining and mentally taxing.

Table 4.1 - Beaufort Wind Scale

Force	Wind Speed (Knots)	Wind	Appearance of Wind Effects On the Water	On Land	Paddling
0	Less than 1	Calm	Sea surface smooth and mirror-like	Calm, smoke rises vertically	Easy paddling
1	1-3	Light Air	Sea rippled, no foam crests	Smoke drift indicates wind direction, still wind vanes	Still easy
2	4-6	Light Breeze	Small wavelets, crests glassy, no breaking	Wind felt on face, leaves rustle, vanes begin to move	Novices will experience weathercocking
3	7-10	Gentle Breeze	Large wavelets, crests begin to break, scattered whitecaps	Leaves and small twigs constantly moving, light flags extended	Good practice for intermediate paddlers
4	11-16	Moderate Breeze	Small waves 1-4 ft. becoming longer, numerous whitecaps	Dust, leaves, and loose paper lifted, small tree branches move	Difficult for novices, may be challenging for intermediates
5	17-21	Fresh Breeze	Moderate waves 4-8 ft taking longer form, many whitecaps, some spray	Small trees in leaf begin to sway	Hard paddling into the wind. Following seas will result in surf rides. Rescues are difficult.
6	22-27	Strong Breeze	Larger waves 8-13 ft, whitecaps common, more spray	Larger tree branches moving, whistling in wires	Small craft warnings. Experienced paddlers only. Very hard paddling into wind. Rescues are very difficult.
7	28-33	Near Gale	Sea heaps up, waves 13-20 ft, white foam streaks off breakers	Whole trees moving, resistance felt walking against wind	Headway is very hard. Very difficult to turn/maneuver. Communication is very difficult. The wind may rip the paddle out of a kayaker's hand.
8	34-40	Gale	Moderately high (13-20 ft) waves of greater length, edges of crests begin to break into spindrift, foam blown in streaks	Whole trees in motion, resistance felt walking against wind	It's every person for themselves. In these conditions you are essentially alone. Rescues are virtually impossible.
9	41-47	Strong Gale	High waves (20 ft), sea begins to roll, dense streaks of foam, spray may reduce visibility	Slight structural damage occurs, slate blows off roofs	Survival paddling. Rescues are impossible.
10	48-55	Storm	Very high waves (20-30 ft) with overhanging crests, sea white with densely blown foam, heavy rolling, lowered visibility	Seldom experienced on land, trees broken or uprooted, "considerable structural damage"	Madness. Running before the wind is about your only option. Pray.
11	56-63	Violent Storm	Exceptionally high (30-45 ft) waves, foam patches cover sea, visibility more reduced		
12	64+	Hurricane	Air filled with foam, waves over 45 ft, sea completely white with driving spray, visibility greatly reduced		

of the wind on the water. This is why small bodies of water are less affected by wind than large expanses of water would be under the same conditions.

The "effects on paddling" column is only intended to give the most general sense of paddling conditions relative to wind. Consider it a "best guess" at what you might encounter.

Bear in mind too that the scale serves as a rough guide only, and conditions will vary depending on geography, local weather conditions, and fetch.

A measurement of wind speed alone however, will not be nearly enough information to make an informed decision about conditions. While it is a primary concern, it is far from the only piece of information that we'll need to plan a kayak outing. Obviously,

wind direction and geography will play a major role too.

For instance, when paddling in sheltered conditions that present minimal fetch and lots of wind breaks (like harbors, sheltered bays and inlets), a force 6 wind may be manageable. On an exposed coast however, the same force 6 wind will be a different experience—imagine a 30 knot wind, blowing offshore and threatening to push you out to sea as you crawl along a totally exposed coast with very few landing possibilities. That's scary!

In my experience, kayakers are very inaccurate when estimating wind speed. We always seem to guess that the wind speed is far higher than what it actually is. I suppose that it just makes for a better story in the pub after a hard day of paddling. A true 25 knots of wind, for example, is an awful lot to handle, and should not be underestimated. Get into the habit of looking up wind speed after a day on the water. The Internet is great for this. It's often easy to consult several automated lighthouse reports, so you can get a good "real world" idea of what wind speed you actually encountered. By doing this post-paddling research on a regular basis, you'll start to have a far better idea of true wind speeds and their effects on the water and your paddling.

A final word of caution about the Beaufort Scale: because it was developed to describe the effects of wind on the open ocean with fully developed seas, it is ultimately better suited to offshore applications than coastal kayaking. As paddlers, we spend the vast majority of our time cruising the coast, an area that the Beaufort scale was not designed to directly address. As always, use caution and conservative judgment when assessing conditions.

Wind and Waves in Opposition

When wind and waves are in opposition, conditions become much more challenging. This applies to both waves created by tidal currents and those created by swell. Of course, this is something that a paddler must take into account when considering a paddling route and that one must continue to monitor and anticipate throughout the day.

For example, when a strong tidal current moves in one direction, creating waves, and powerful winds blow in the opposite direction, the wind will cause waves to "stand up" more and be much more likely to break. Extremely challenging conditions can result. Furthermore, tides change and tidal currents reverse their flow, which means that depending on the situation, conditions can improve or deteriorate dramatically.

Likewise, waves from ocean swell will also be steeper if they are opposed by strong wind. For example, a shore break's waves will become steeper and break with more force if a brisk offshore breeze is blowing against them.

Dealing with Head Winds

When the sea's asleep, we can go most places we want. But even when the sea is just starting to wake up, things get pretty dynamic. The wind picks up and waves crash and surge. Once the sea is fully awake, forget it—we have no business whatsoever thinking that we can survive the ocean when it's in full motion, let alone tame it.

Obviously, a headwind is going to slow a kayak down, and a tailwind is going to help push it on its way. But it's pretty hard to guess what actual difference in traveling speed will result from the action of the wind. Not having a reasonable estimate of speed made good will make your navigation far less accurate.

Fortunately, another table has been created to help estimate the effect that wind will have on the forward progress of a sea kayak.

Training for headwinds.

Table 4.2 - Effect of Wind on Forward Progress

Wind Speed	Headwind Resistance	Tailwind Assistance
0 knots	0 knots	0 knots
5 knots	-0.5 knots	0 knots
10 knots	-1 knots	+1 knots
15 knots	-1.5 knots	+1.5 knots
20 knots	-2 knots	+2 knots
25 knots	-3 knots	+2.5 knots

As usual, Table 4.2 is intended solely as a rough guide to cruising speeds. The numbers were generated based on a forward speed of 3 knots per hour. Something to keep in mind is that as a tailwind builds, so do waves at the stern. A following sea will often make it possible to pick up surf rides that will provide far more speed than the push from the wind at our backs could generate.

Different paddlers counsel different strategies for dealing with a headwind. One old chestnut is to slow down and "conserve energy" for what will be a long arduous slog. Let's do a little math and see what numbers we get.

As we can see from Table 4.3, slowing down a mere 1/2 knot to "conserve energy" will slow us down quite a bit. With 15 knots of headwind, if we slow down from 3 knots to 2.5 knots, our speed made good will be approximately 1 nautical mile (about 1.9 km) per hour. That means that to cover 6 miles, it will take 6 hours.

Conversely, if we paddle at 3.5 knots, speeding up a 1/2 knot from 3, we'll achieve a speed made good closer to 2 knots. This will put us in camp in 3 hours, or exactly half the time it took paddling at 2.5 knots.

So the question posed is this: who has conserved more energy? One paddler will poke along for 6 hours. The other will paddle aggressively for 3, put up a tent, have a meal, and maybe even take a little nap. Who is more rested?

You decide—plug different numbers into Table 4.3, and see what kind of times will be generated by inputting different distances, winds and cruising speeds. You'll find that when the wind blows in your face, in order to save energy in the long term it is better to respond by paddling aggressively, rather than slowing down. The same is true for currents or any other conditions that may counter your progress. Of course there comes a point when the wind will be so strong that paddling against it just isn't worth the effort.

Table 4.3 - Effect of Headwind on Paddling Speed

Wind Speed	Speed Made Good	Time Paddling to Cover 6 Nautical Miles
Based on 2.5 knot paddling speed		
0 knots	2.5 - 0 = 2.5 knots	2.4 hrs
5 knots	2.5 - 0.5 = 2 knots	3 hrs
10 knots	2.5 - 1 = 1.5 knots	4 hrs
15 knots	2.5 - 1.5 = 1 knots	6 hrs
20 knots	2.5 - 2 = 0.5 knots	12 hrs
Based on 3 knot paddling speed		
0 knots	3 - 0 = 3 knots	2 hrs
5 knots	3 - 0.5 = 2.5 knots	2.4 hrs
10 knots	3 - 1 = 2 knots	3 hrs
15 knots	3 - 1.5 = 1.5 knots	4 hrs
20 knots	3 - 2 = 1 knots	6 hrs
Based on 3.5 knot paddling speed		
0 knots	3.5 - 0 = 3.5 knots	1.72 hrs
5 knots	3.5 - 0.5 = 3 knots	2 hrs
10 knots	3.5 - 1 = 2.5 knots	2 hrs
15 knots	3.5 - 1.5 = 2 knots	3 hrs
20 knots	3.5 - 2 = 1.5 knots	4 hrs

Paddling along side a magnificent fin whale - the 2nd largest animal on earth next to the blue whale.

Down-Wind Runs

Every now and again the unthinkable occurs and you encounter a tail wind, pushing you in the exact direction that you want to go. Ah, bliss!

With the wind at your back, paddling is a treat, and you'll cover an amazing amount of distance quickly. If the wind is strong enough and there's enough fetch, waves will begin to form. This is known as a following sea. Swell will be rolling up behind you, lifting and dropping your boat as the waves steam by. When conditions are right, the waves will be steep enough to be surfed.

Once waves start to form and get steep enough that kayaks begin to accelerate down the faces, it's very easy to tell competent and assured surfers from less-experienced paddlers. While the more novice kayakers will be back-paddling in order to avoid surfing down a wave, experienced paddlers will be leaning forward from the waist and sprinting hard in order to lock onto a good ride.

Following seas and the resulting waves can provide an amazing boost of speed. There is nothing quite like being a mile offshore, and catching a ride on a wind wave or swell. On the right day, you can surf the wave until it dissipates, and sprint for the next one behind it, linking multiple rides together. It's an awesome feeling and the amount of ground that can be covered in a short time is remarkable. Just bear in mind that it will be a long hard paddle home if you have to turn around and retrace your route to get back to the same launch site.

Down-wind "shuttle runs" are great. This requires the transport of at least two vehicles. Both are driven to the take-out, where one is left behind (along with a change of clothes and hot drinks etc.), while the other vehicle shuttles paddlers, boats and gear to the put-in. With this arrangement, you can drive to one good put-in, paddle downwind along the coast, and still have a vehicle at the takeout. To some it may seem like cheating, but only having to paddle one way, with the wind, is more like a dream come true to me.

Surfing ocean swell is so exhilarating that it's very easy to focus exclusively on the wave behind you and catching the next ride. In other words, it's a cinch to lose track of paddling partners. Once kayakers are locking onto rides, they will tend to get very spread out very quickly. It's important to be mindful of this and to make sure that you all stay in touch and keep an eye on one another.

Dealing with Beam (Side) Winds

The toughest wind conditions to deal with are generated when the wind is coming from the side. Whether perpendicular to the kayak or blowing from a more oblique angle, a strong wind will grab and pull at a paddler, threatening to throw them off balance. At 25 knots and above it's hard to control the paddle, because the top blade will act like a weathervane. It's best to drop the paddle as low as possible in really high winds, opting for a very low stroke angle in order to hide the paddle from the wind and minimize how much surface area of your upper blade is presented to gusts. Bending low at the waist and virtually dropping your chest on the fore deck will also reduce the surface area of your upper body that the wind can act upon. Above 25 knots, if you present the top paddle blade to the wind, you risk having it torn from your grip—or even worse, if you do hold on to it, powerful gusts can lash the upper blade and be extremely destabilizing or knock you over. With a constant wind it is easier to balance the effect of side winds than if it is gusting. With a constant wind you'll find yourself leaning into the wind, but gusts will grab at you unexpectedly and lulls between gusts will have you falling over, making staying upright a real balancing act.

Wind coming from an angle will also affect your boat's ability to hold a course. All kayaks should be designed to "weathercock".

Weathercocking is the tendency of a boat to turn into the wind. This should be a relatively modest effect. Kayaks that do not weathercock, and turn downwind instead are liabilities because they are almost impossible to turn upwind—a very scary proposition if that happens to be the direction that you need to go. The best kayaks feel very neutral with only modest weathercocking, even in high winds, so course correction can be done with edging and strokes. To keep a straight course, this will mean paddling with your boat slightly tilted into the wind. Your forward stroke on the windward side will also be more of a sweeping forward stroke. In fact, in strong beam winds, your windward strokes will be more like sweeping braces since your boat should be tilted to that same side and the combination of wind and waves will make staying balanced tricky. Weathercocking can also be balanced out by deploying a skeg or rudder. Skegs and rudders are deployed to

A kayak's tendency to turn into the wind (weathercock) can be controlled by deploying a skeg or rudder.

control the stern of a kayak.

A common misconception is that a skeg has two settings: up and down. The reality is that a skeg can be deployed to any level. When up, the skeg will not affect the kayak's tendency to weathercock. When deployed, the skeg will hold the stern in place and allow the bow to be blown downwind. The further down a skeg is deployed, the more it will hold the stern in place and therefore, the more powerfully it will fight the natural weathercocking characteristics of your kayak. This means that you'll need to play around with how much you deploy your skeg in order to find a happy medium, where the influence of the wind is cancelled out.

The wind will also build sea conditions, so you'll also need to contend with waves coming at you on an angle. If you have waves and wind coming in from the side, keeping your course becomes even more difficult. If the waves are big enough, tilt your boat into them and brace at the same time, while staying loose at the hips and letting your boat "go with the flow".

Turning a Kayak in Wind

Turning a kayak in strong wind can be tricky. Although the natural weathercocking characteristics of your kayak will help you turn upwind, it's not a quick process. In order to make the quickest turns, you'll want to use a combination of forward and reverse sweeps. The reverse sweep in particular will be very effective. Something else to consider is that in windy conditions, waves are often present. The peak of a wave is a great place to turn your kayak, because a portion of your bow and/or stern will be clear of the water, resulting in less drag and a faster turn.

Paddling in High Winds

In high winds, the biggest concern is the surface area that you present for the wind to catch. Low decks minimize the effects of wind. High decks and bulky gear strapped to the outside of a boat act almost like sails. For this reason, keep clean decks with gear

stowed in hatches. Similarily, as mentioned earlier, you'll want your body and paddle to present the minimal surface area possible for the wind to act upon. Stay low in your kayak and keep your paddle blade extra low on the windward side of your kayak.

In really high winds, the only course of action is to get off the water as quickly as possible, or at least sprint into the most protected area available. When strong winds start to blow, there is a lag before sea conditions catch up and build to the same ferocity. In the very early stages of a gale, the sea state is not a problem at all, but the wind will knock you over without any assistance from waves. So when the wind starts to build seriously, get off the water.

If you are on shore, watching a storm build to epic proportions, stay there! Never leave a place of safety for a place of greater safety. It is faulty logic. Stay safely where you are and hunker down to watch the storm. Secure all gear, tether your boat to a tree or some other anchor, secure your tent thoroughly with guy lines and place a nice round melon-sized rock in each corner.

Wind can be a very frustrating thing to deal with. It can really slow your progress or even stop it cold. Really high winds are more than frustrating; they can be absolutely terrifying. More to the point, they can be deadly. Storm-force winds blowing offshore will blast a paddler out to sea. Even if the kayaker can manage to stay upright for a time, they will be unable to attain the safety of shore or shelter, and be driven to sea. Conditions will only worsen further out to sea, away from whatever minimal shelter is provided by the coastline. Caught out on the water in this scenario, there is virtually no possibility of rescue or survival.

Onshore and Offshore Breezes

On otherwise calm, warm days, wind will still be generated because the warming and cooling rates of the ocean and land aren't the same.

Over the course of the day, land will warm faster than a large body of water. As warm air rises off the land, the cooler air out over the water flows in. The result is a light breeze that blows onshore from the sea.

At night, the reverse happens. Land cools faster, while the water retains heat longer, so the cool air over the land rushes out across the water, creating a light breeze coming off the land and blowing offshore to the sea.

Katabatic and Anabatic Winds

Katabatic and anabatic winds are created by differences in temperature and they can be incredibly fierce. As different air masses heat and cool down independently, the differential in temperature generates a lot of air movement between the two, and

thus, high winds. These effects grow in intensity as the differences in temperature increase. Wind speeds are also magnified by geographical features like steep valley walls and confined inlets and fjords, which will funnel wind and generate even stronger gusts.

Anabatic winds are created when inlets and valleys warm up during the day. Warm air travels up the steep walls of the inlet and into the mountains, where it meets the colder air at higher elevation.

Katabatic winds occur in the evening and night as the colder air at elevation sweeps down out of the mountains and into valleys and inlets.

These winds can make otherwise ideal seeming campsites very blustery and cold. It's not uncommon for katabatic winds in prime locations to hit speeds of 60 knots and above!

Gap Winds

Gap winds are generated in areas where wind is channeled through gaps, like passages between the coast and an island. Just like water flowing through a narrow opening, wind will accelerate when forced through a small passage. Gap winds also occur when onshore wind funnels through valleys or other lowlands in a peninsula. Strong winds will blow through the opening and out the other side into the inlet, resulting in sudden and powerful winds at a very localized point on the inner shore.

Local Weather Patterns

Although it's impossible to predict wind conditions with perfect accuracy, there are usually some common wind themes in an area, and it's worth asking the locals about them.

Because winds can be so localized due to specific geography, marine forecasts may not reflect the conditions that you will encounter in one specific place. Even really high winds that are only prevailing over a very small area will not necessarily get a mention in the forecast. Again, it's local knowledge that will come

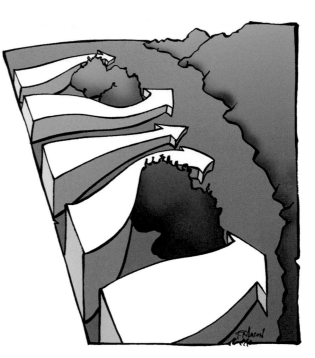

Gap winds funnel through passages and over lowlands, resulting in sudden and powerful winds in very localized areas.

to your rescue. Read guidebooks and talk to local fishers and sailors. If they live or work in the area, they will know all the bad spots. If you tell them that you're in a kayak, they'll be especially thrilled to tell you about all the nasty areas that can kill you.

Sometimes you can use prevailing weather patterns to your advantage. Because onshore winds consistently tend to pick up in the afternoon, you'll want to paddle out of an inlet in the early morning in order to avoid a headwind. Conversely, you wait until the afternoon before paddling back down the inlet, so you get the help of a nice tailwind.

All in all, it's invariably a good idea to get a very early start when trying to avoid wind. In most locations, winds arc lighter in the early morning and have a tendency to build in intensity as the day wears on. Always consult marine weather forecasts, keep your eyes and ears open for changing conditions, and pay particular heed to areas that have a bad reputation for high wind events.

Forecasts and Geography

Marine forecasts are an invaluable tool for assessing route plans and the likelihood of fierce winds. Pay special attention to wind direction relative to geography and currents. Some areas are notorious for funneling winds, while other locations may feature landscape that can provide shelter in the lee of a storm. Wind will also radically change the character of waves in the surf zone and tidal rapids.

Storms can blow up incredibly quickly in many areas, and water is a very inhospitable place when the wind howls. So even on day trips in places you know well, be ready to get off the water in a hurry. A lack of respect for the potential of wind acting on water is a huge mistake. A sense of complacency around water can get you killed, regardless of paddling skill. Never underestimate the ability of strong winds to transform your favorite mellow paddling route into a scary struggle to stay upright and survive. Everyone's comfort level is different, but having paddled in winds hitting 35 knots and above, I can confidently state that I don't enjoy it one bit and am not at all keen to repeat the experience.

Finally, always check your gut. If you are experiencing doubts, or just have a feeling that things aren't quite right, bag the mission.

A maelstrom of wind and water – exciting paddling conditions!

There'll be other days to paddle. Be very conservative when it comes to wind and water. The sheer power of gales and storms dwarfs any kayaker's abilities. It is madness to seek to conquer the sea. We must, instead, adapt, conform, and respond to the water's moods and whims. Only with this mentality can we hope to find safe passage.

RESCUES IN WIND

Wind generates monumental changes in marine conditions, and any craft traveling across the surface of water is subject to the ferocious forces of storms and gales.

Rescues in high winds are very difficult. Any loose gear not properly tethered will be quickly blown away from a capsized kayak and likely lost for good. The wind will grab and tear at paddles and paddlers alike, making maneuvering both very tricky and exhausting. Should a swimmer become separated from their kayak or paddle, even for a moment, they may very well be unable to swim fast enough to reestablish contact with their equipment. Likewise, buoyant gear like paddle floats will be blown away across the water in the blink of an eye.

For this reason, it is highly desirable for a swimmer to position themselves downwind from their kayak. This way the boat will tend to be blown toward them and back into their grasp should they momentarily lose contact.

One of the greatest challenges in high winds is simply to communicate with others. Even at extremely close range, the howl of the wind will snatch words away and deafen ears. It is incredibly frustrating to be bellowing at someone who is only a few feet away and still be unable to make oneself understood. In these conditions, it becomes even more important that all members of the group know their roles in the rescue process and be well practiced and confident in their execution.

Ultimately, the only sensible course of action when encountering really high winds on the water is to head for shore and shelter as fast as possible.

SEA KAYAKING
ROUGH WATERS

BY ALEX MATTHEWS

Dear Kayak,

I know you don't want to hear this.
But I met another kayak. It's not you.
It's just that the Chatham makes me
feel so confident, so safe. Is it the
hull? The lines? I'm not sure. I just
know that I'm doing things I never
thought were possible. I hope we'll
stay in touch.

Bill

P.S. I'm giving you to my Uncle
Terrence. Don't hate me.

www.neckykayaks.com

CHATHAM™
Designed to inspire confidence.

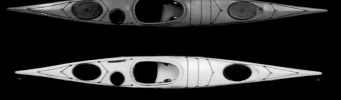

Available in plastic, fiberglass or advanced composite, the
16', 17' or 18' Chatham has just about everything you'd want in
a kayak, including tremendous maneuverability that never sacrifices
stability. But its best feature may be making you
the paddler you've always claimed to be.

JOHNSON
OUTDOORS

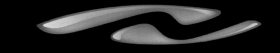

NECKY KAYAKS

FROM MILD...

...TO WILD

©GaryandJoanieMcGuffin.com

Get into the water with the most comprehensive line of paddle sports clothing for men, women and children.

Kōkatat
watersports wear

www.kokatat.com

Waterproof, breathable fabric.	Waterproof, breathing.
Curved, water-resistant RF welded zippers.	No zippers.
Designed for easier movement.	Doesn't move much.
Inner latex neck seal.	Uh...Littleneck.
Prevents clammy feeling.	Always feels clammy.

Tech Wear from the world's most trusted PFD makers.

Extrasport introduces the most comfortable, protective dry wear you can buy. Dry Tops, Splash Tops and Paddling Pant that'll leave no one feeling clammy except our competitors.

first in comfort™

Also features: Glideskin™ TI-coat adjustable neck closure for added comfort and easy on and off
• Stretch fabric panels for free motion • Comfortable dual closure wrist protection • Reflective piping
*Mid Semi-Dry Top shown

www.extrasport.com

JOHNSON OUTDOORS

Kayak in the Cape Breton Highlands!

North River Kayak Tours
www.NorthRiverKayak.com

Eagle North Canoe & Kayak Tours
www.Kayakingcapebreton.ca

Cape Breton Sea Coast Adventures
www.members.tripod.com/adventure_4u

Ingonish Chalets
Cozy Pine Log Chalets and Suites
nestled in the Cape Breton Highlands.
www.IngonishChalets.com

Mermaid's Purse Farm
Bed & Breakfast and Gallery

The perfect base for your adventure on the coast of Maine.

Great paddling, wandering, or just relaxing. Flexible arrangements and good food. Open all year.
We look forward to making you feel at home!

Visit our website, call, or email for details.

 The Mermaid's Purse Farm
50 Lighthouse Point Road, PO Box 208, Prospect Harbor, Maine 04669
207 963 7344, www.mermaidspursefarm.com, mermaids@midmaine.com

"Slick."

**The new Turn Lock Coupler (TLC)
from Aqua-Bound**

No tools, no holes, no hassles.

**The new Turn Lock Coupler (TLC) adjustable ferrule system from
Aqua-Bound allows for multiple feather angles and is incredibly
simple to use. In 2007 it will be standard on our carbon abX line of
RAY SERIES paddles.**

Weight. Less.

Aqua-Bound

www.aquabound.com

If you enjoyed this book, be sure to check out this DVD

The Ultimate Guide to
Sea Kayaking

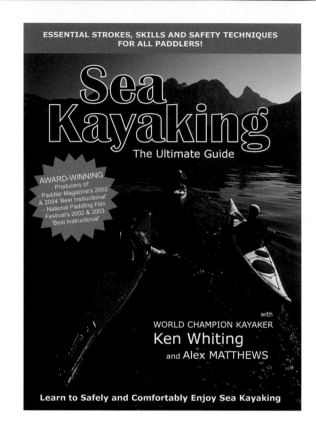

A four-part video by World Champion Kayaker, Ken Whiting, and expert sea kayaker, Alex Matthews, which provides both new and experienced paddlers with the knowledge and skills necessary to safely and comfortably enjoy touring and sea kayaking.

PART ONE introduces new paddlers to the sport, to the equipment that gets used, and to important issues to understand before you hit the water.

PART TWO focuses on the Essential strokes and techniques.

PART THREE looks exclusively at safety and rescue techniques.

PART FOUR deals with more advanced paddling techniques, such as preparing for multi-day trips, and dealing with such things as surf, current, and weather.

OVER 2 HOURS OF INSTRUCTION!

$29.95 US, $39.95 CAN

AWARD WINNING
Waterwalker Film Festival

"Great video. Terrific Instruction!"
- TOON, EDITOR, KAYAK SESSION MAGAZINE

"Fantastic Video!
I watch it over and over!"
- MORRIS ILYNIAK, TORONTO, ONTARIO

Available at your local outdoor store, book store, on the web at
www.helipress.com, or by phone **1-888-582-2001**